Coin collecting 101: What you

Coin collecting
101
What you
need to know

DATE DUE

©2005 KP Books
Published by

kp books
An Imprint of F+W Publications

700 East State Street • Iola, WI 54990-0001
715-445-2214 • 888-457-2873

Our toll-free number to place an order or obtain
a free catalog is (800) 258-0929.

Library of Congress Catalog Number: 2005906840

ISBN: 0-89689-182-8

Designed by Elizabeth Krogwold

Edited by Todd Haefer

Printed in The United States of America

Contents

Preview

A general view of a coin bourse.

So, you want to be a coin collector? Good! If you go at it the right way, you can look forward to years of enjoyment of a hobby that is nearly as old as the first coins on this planet. Coin collecting is a hobby, but it's also big business, with millions of dollars changing hands every day.

Right now, you are traveling down one of two roads toward this hobby. Either you never have collected coins in your life, or you have begun to collect and are looking for advice as to the next steps. I've tried, as I wrote this book, to anticipate the questions you will have, regardless of what attracted your interest. There won't be room for all the answers, but I'll try to steer you in the directions that will contain the information.

It won't be easy. Coin collectors have their own special rules, such as "Don't clean your coins!" - and most daunting, their own special terms, symbols and abbreviations. Like almost every hobby, they have a secret language that must become part of your learning curve before you can lean back and enjoy your status as a collector of money.

My job would be far easier if coin collecting was a simple, one-topic hobby. Numismatics - a four-syllable word (NEW-mis-MAT-ics) that nobody can spell, much less pronounce - covers virtually every conceivable form of money, including, but not limited, to bars of soap and dog teeth. Thus a collector of dog teeth could be considered a numismatist (new-MIS-ma-TIST). Notice that the emphasis is on the second and fourth syllables, while (NEW-mis-MAT-ics) has the accent on the first and third syllables.

Expediency has taken many available objects and turned them into money for other uses. Wampum, woodpecker scalps, porcelain - you name it and at some time, somewhere, it probably has been used for money.

Anything that got missed in cramming all these collectibles under one heading winds up in a close relative - exonumia.

Coins, tokens, medals, paper money, siege money, wooden money, scrip, checks and dozens of other categories of collectibles come under one general heading - numismatics. To save time as you go through this book, I'll refer to coin collecting, but you will understand that some of what you read applies to all those other forms of money.

If it is starting to dawn on you that there's more than meets the eye in coin collecting, you've gotten my point. As you will see, besides dozens of collectible forms of money, there are literally thousands of different ways to form a collection. That part is up to you. One of the most common forms of bad advice that you will get is someone telling you that you "must" collect such and such. The good advice is to collect things that you enjoy, that you like and that you want to keep. Above all, it's your choice. Otherwise, what's the fun of collecting something you are told to collect?

That doesn't mean that from time to time you will see or hear advice on what not to collect. I won't stop you, but if you don't take advice seriously, your collecting interests may wind up in a dead end. I use the analogy of a sandy beach. You're welcome to collect sand, by the bucketful. But no matter how much sand you collect, you won't begin to see any return other than filling that large sandbox in the backyard. There are dead ends in coin collecting just like any other hobby, so don't be afraid to accept advice.

I'm going to repeat things. It's not that I forget that I've written some advice, it's just that I'm stressing important points that will help teach you the many pleasures and pitfalls of collecting. When you see advice the second or third time, it will reinforce what you read the first time.

There's plenty more of my good advice in the coming pages. I've been writing about coin collecting and answering questions from collectors for nearly 40 years. I know the pitfalls and the triumphs that you are likely to find along your path. The whole idea of this book is to help you enjoy coin collecting.

One of the nice things about coin collecting as a hobby is that most of your coins are going to retain their face value, so if for some reason you decide to end your collecting, you can still spend the coins. Most values are going to go up. Some right away, some not for a century or two, but if you play your cards right, you will ultimately profit from a well-kept coin collection.

A childhood fascination can last a lifetime.

Foreword

By David C. Harper

David C. Harper

If you are looking for a five-minute course that will change your life, put this book down and walk to the fluff aisle. Better yet, buy a video where good-looking people tell you how great you are, or fly to Las Vegas and marry a total stranger on the spur of the moment. Coin collecting is not for you.

On the other hand, if you consider yourself to be a curious sort who likes to peel away layers like an onion to get to the nub of an issue, you might just find coin collecting to be one of the best things ever. It changed my life. I made my first tentative steps down the coin-collecting road when I was 8 years old. More than four decades later, I am still walking that road. Coin collecting gave me an absorbing hobby. What I learned from it gave me a leg up in school and ultimately gave me a career, which was a heck of a leg up in life.

That's how I came to know Alan Herbert, the author of this book. When you work with someone for 27 years, you get to know his motivation, as well as what he is capable of. Alan would like nothing better than to give you a thorough grounding in coin collecting. Take the opportunity. He is a master and you don't have to fly to Tibet to study at his feet. You can make coin collecting a family project and share it with your kids or grandkids. Or, you can make coin collecting a hobby that can be your very own escape from the world without another person or problem to bother you. It is your choice. You set the agenda. You choose the setting. You choose your level of involvement. But no fluff.

On the top 10 list of ways to lose money, the No. 1 item is spending five minutes on coin collecting and then assuming you have learned all you need to know. There are sellers on the Internet just waiting for this kind of person.

Open your mind. Consider the possibility that you don't even know what a coin is. Most people call any metallic disc with a design on it a coin. That may suffice in daily life, but to coin collectors what makes those discs coins is whether they are spendable now, or ever were spendable at any place of business. Discs that meet those criteria are coins. Discs that don't meet those criteria might be tokens, medals, buttons or just castoffs from a machine shop die-punching machine.

This book is designed to help you move comfortably into a hobby that is not a fad. It is the opposite of a fad. It has roots dating back to the 14th-century Renaissance in northern Italy and was a documented activity right at the founding of the U.S. Mint, when Lord St. Oswald obtained some new issues of the United States in 1794 (which his heirs sold for a pretty penny two centuries later). Collectors can count on the fact that this hobby has a permanence that gives them confidence to act. Collectors of silver dollars who will someday retire from the hobby know that a generation from now, other collectors of silver dollars will be there to buy whenever they are ready to sell. In the end, it is this permanence that is the substantial underlying guarantee of the hobby. Now you probably have a question that you always wanted to ask. Hold it for now. The odds are it will be addressed in one of the chapters. If it hasn't been answered by the time you have finished this book, you will probably have a better idea of who to ask to get an appropriate answer.

At the root of coin collecting is an indefinable impulse some people have to simply own coins for their own sake and in consequence learn everything that is knowable about them. There is also a profit motive. No coin collector I ever met said he began the hobby to lose money. Sometimes money can be lost, but it is tuition to the college of hobby life. If you pay attention to your lessons, you get it all back and much more. You get the enjoyment of the hobby and the attendant health and lifestyle benefits. If you are like me, you might even earn your living with what you learn here. Opportunities are almost infinite.

Still reading? Good. You've passed the first test. Now turn the page and get on with this great hobby.

David C. Harper is the editor of Numismatic News, World Coin News *and* Bank Note Reporter, *three of the periodicals that F+W Publications publishes for the numismatic hobby.*

1794 Flowing Hair dollar

Introduction

Alan Herbert

Do you have an interest in, or appreciate art, history, sociology, geography or any of a score of other disciplines? Coins can match you, interest for interest. Almost every recent coin carries the bust of some historic person from our past, as just one example of what coins can teach you.

History. Ah, history. I flunked world history my freshman year in high school. I could see absolutely no use for facts about wars and revolutions and kings and dictators - especially several thousand years ago. I argued - unsuccessfully - with the teacher, who refused to see my point. Little did either of us know that I would be using dates and history almost every day of my career in coin collecting. It was the subject, not the teacher. Same teacher, same year - earth science - and I got a 95 grade for the year. (I almost became a geologist.)

Starting a coin collection usually isn't something that you plan in advance. More often than not you will find a coin or a token or medal that catches your eye. As you study a newly discovered coin and learn more about it, you probably will find that it fits with other, similar pieces that go with your original find.

You also might be the fortunate one who inherits a group or collection of coins. Resist the urge to immediately go out and sell the coins. Unless you are on the edge of bankruptcy, you will be far better off to hang onto them until you have had a chance to study and evaluate them.

Coins can turn up in some strange places. I found an 1895 nickel laying in the middle of the road at a drill site at an old gold mine. A woman on a ghost town tour in the Black Hills of South Dakota found a Barber half dollar lying at her feet. The stories of such discoveries are to be found throughout the history of our country. Anyone with a metal detector can give you chapter and verse on such finds.

One important point. There are several written and unwritten definitions of a collection. The most frequently used is the one that describes a collection as an orderly grouping of coins in a series, denomination, metal or type. The much broader definition - one that old-time collectors have trouble with - is any group of coins that are saved and NOT used for their monetary value to buy things.

As a collector, you are likely to be snubbed by some of the purists who own a complete collection of some elusive and expensive series. Their idea of collecting is competing with other collectors for the finest known this or that. They are also the ones most likely to order you to collect some specific group of coins. Fortunately they are a tiny minority in the

1901S half dollar

A coin album

hobby and usually can safely be ignored.

There are cliques like this in antique collecting, art collecting or any other hobby.

Actually, your collection can consist of a single coin. That statement pushes the traditional boundaries of a coin collection pretty hard and won't set well with many traditional collectors. However, in many, many cases, a collection does start with a single coin. Another division is between the passive and the active collector. You may sit for years with a special coin or two, or even a full-scale collection, without doing anything further. An active collector will keep looking at those coins and wonder whether he can find some more coins to add to what he or she has. Passive or active, you are still both collectors.

Here's an example for you from my personal collecting experience. I brought home a Lowenbrau beer glass from Germany in 1987. My one-glass collection remained dormant until 2000. I decided to see if I could find some other beer glasses and mugs with brand names. In five years, my collection is nearing the 1,200-item mark. It even resurrected my childhood interest in HO-gauge electric trains, when I found that there are freight cars with beer logos on them. That branch of my collection is up to a 35-car beer train.

Getting back to coins. The most popular question in coin collecting is one shared by other hobbies - "What's it worth?

If you've ever put on a yard or garage sale, you know how difficult it is to put a price on items that have served you in one way or another for years. You are guessing as to what customers will be willing to pay. Unless you put on commercial yard sales, your whole pricing structure is guesswork, but after a few sales you will know the market much better.

The same applies to a collection you inherit. Even if the prices paid are marked on the coin holders - a sign of a knowledgeable collector - you have no way of knowing whether today's market is above or below

2 x 2 holder with collector notations and price paid.

The North American Coins and Prices *book is a good reference guide.*

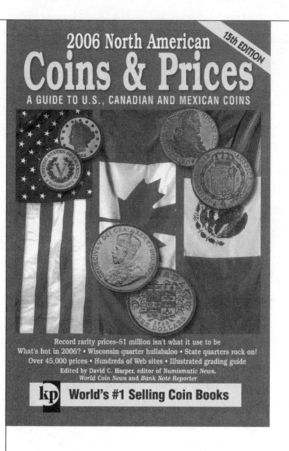

2006 North American

Coins & Prices

15th EDITION

A GUIDE TO U.S., CANADIAN AND MEXICAN COINS

Record rarity prices–$1 million isn't what it use to be
What's hot in 2006? • Wisconsin quarter hullabaloo • State quarters rock on!
Over 45,000 prices • Hundreds of Web sites • Illustrated grading guide
Edited by David C. Harper, editor of Numismatic News,
World Coin News and Bank Note Reporter

kp World's #1 Selling Coin Books

that figure. Before selling a single coin either get an appraisal or learn for yourself what the coins are actually worth.

There are several price guides, including F+W Publications' *North American Coins and Prices* and *Coin Prices* magazine. You will need to learn about grading your coins before the guides will make sense. One day, if the process continues, you may decide to keep the collection and actively search for companion pieces. Later, as you add to the group, you will find that you have in fact become an active collector.

The typical American coin accumulation.

Many collections begin as coins that, for one reason or another, are simply lying about the house, or are hiding in an old sock or purse. Converting a random group into a collection takes knowledge and a fair amount of work - and money. This book is intended to outline most of the areas where you will have questions or need advice.

Remember that this is an outline. You start from here and find the sources of information that you want for your particular interests. If I were to fill in all the gaps, list every information source, define every term, you'd have a shelf full of books this size. There are tremendous quantities of information out there. All you need to do is get motivated to go find it.

As with any activity, there are misunderstandings and misconceptions. One very common mistake is to assume, because one date in a series or denomination is quite valuable, that all the coins in that group are equally as valuable. Another common mistake is to misread a price chart and automatically assume that your coin is at the top end of the range, despite being well worn or even damaged.

Curiosity comes at several levels. As a collector, you need at least some form of curiosity. Whether it's a desire to know everything there is to know about your latest buy or a real need to spend hours researching your whole collection, curiosity is a trait that helps make you an experienced collector. Ultimately, it will pay off in added value for your favorite pieces. Cultivate your curiosity. Ask questions. A growing collection will add to your knowledge in many ways.

A collection can be as simple or as complex as you want it to be. But the advice to "walk before you run" applies here. One of the quickest ways to get in over your head is to be a checkbook collector, buying everything in sight. Without a plan, your haphazard collection is just that. Even if your collection isn't fully organized, you are still a collector. You will find a more detailed discussion in the chapter on Buying and Selling.

Ask questions. I can't repeat that often enough. It's a key step to fully enjoying your collection. New collectors usually ask some of the same questions, so there are some that I have answered hundreds, if not thousands of times. The approach to the question is often different, even if the answer is the same, so it never gets boring. I learn from each question and I will attempt to impart that knowledge as you proceed through each chapter. Remember, and repeat often, "There are no dumb questions."

I should point out that my advice is not limited to the beginning or novice collector. There are a number of important points that even experienced collectors have neglected or forgotten that this book will bring to mind. On some points, my advice may differ from that of other authors, a controversy that you may want to dig into a bit deeper. Much has changed in the hobby in the last two or three decades and some earlier books may reflect outmoded or obsolete practices or terms that you probably will want to avoid.

There are exceptions to fit every rule, so a good thing to learn is to beware of the nitpickers. My answers to questions are couched in general terms, but there's always one spoilsport who has to show his importance by questioning the answer as it applies to his own little niche. Corrections or constructive criticism are always welcome, because that's how I learn, too.

You will find that almost every chapter has at least one important message. Some have several, so you will probably refer to this book from time to time as you progress in the hobby. The point here is to have fun as you learn. That's what a hobby is for.

Chapter 1

HISTORY AND THE MINTING PROCESS

Bronze Sestertius of Roman Emperor Hadrian (117-138 AD).

Coins have been around for a long time. Their use in commerce and trade began about 700 B.C., with some evidence that crude forms were in use even earlier. The Chinese beat the Western world to coins and paper money by at least several hundred years.

Q: *I have a reeded edge 1909 cent. Is this a pattern?*

A: *Sorry, but it's an alteration. No modern reeded cents or nickels were ever issued from the U.S. Mint.*

Byzantine Gold Solidus featuring Christ and Constantinople.

Crude is the catchword for much of the earliest coinage. Copper and even wood were used to make dies. The first designs were simple punch marks. The Romans and Greeks did much to advance coin designs that gradually changed from rough outlines to detailed figures that often reflected the hair and clothing styles of the era.

The period from about 500 A.D. to 1500 is considered to be the Medieval era. Coin designs deteriorated for much of that span. Specialized minting processes were lost or forgotten. Jetons, a form of token, came into use, mostly for accounting purposes. At the end of the Medieval period, coinage emerged with new vigor. The French introduced new methods in the 1550s that brought about significant changes in the appearance of coins.

The earliest coins were made by fixing a die, placing a planchet on it, the opposing die on top and the stack struck with a heavy hammer, giving the name "hammered coins" to the product. Mechanical coin presses eventually replaced the hammer and for the first time produced coins that were as alike as the proverbial peas in a pod.

Modern coinage methods draw on the earlier methods, but a hammer man would never recognize today's coin presses, some of which are capable of spitting out 750 coins per minute. Reaching those speeds has benefited some of the larger mints, such as the four U.S. mints currently operating, but it has put some smaller mints out of business.

The minting process is quite complicated, until you break it down into its three main components - planchets, dies and striking. Planchets are the material - usually a metal or alloy - upon which the coin is struck. The dies carry the design and apply the designs for both sides onto the planchet, making it a coin. Striking, as I've already noted, has progressed from the hammer to the high-speed coin press.

Planchets are made in a two-step process. Long strips of coin metal are run through blanking presses that drive multiple blunt punches through the strip, punching as many as a dozen blanks from the strip at each stroke. As you can imagine, this is a very noisy process and even though the blanking press is usually mounted right on bedrock, it shakes the building.

The blanks are passed through an upsetting mill that turns the edge of the blank back, creating a raised area of coin metal where the design rim will be on the struck coin. This upsetting turns the blank into a planchet. The two terms are often misused as a single term, "blank planchet," but the two are distinctly different stages.

Q: *Why was the eagle selected as the principal symbol on our early coins?*

A: *Coin designers had a difficult time, as many people were illiterate. It was common practice to describe a coin by naming it for the prominent central design or device. The eagle went on our first gold coins to give the public a symbol that was readily identified and was distinctly different from the Spanish pillar dollar, which was the principal coin of commerce.*

The law is quite vague, specifying only that an eagle be depicted, without establishing the size. The apparent intent was to give the designer as wide a latitude as possible. There is also no specification that the eagle be a bald eagle, but that has become a matter of tradition.

Original coin dies

Coin metals are chosen for their ready availability, their cost and their ability to accept the intended design and to allow it to be applied to huge numbers of coins with minimal wear on the dies. The most common coin metal is copper, while nickel, iron, zinc, silver and gold and several other metals have all been used, usually in an alloy, or mixture of two or more metals. I'll discuss more of the coin-metal specifications in the chapters on the different denominations of U.S. coins.

Most of today's dies are made by the hubbing method. The hub is a tool that has the design in relief, just as it appears on the coin. A master hub or master die is made by a reducing lathe, a machine

Janvier reducing machine transfers the larger model to the actual-size die used to strike the coin.

that copies a plastic model, reducing it to the actual coin size and cutting it on the face of the hub or die. The master die, in turn, is used to make working hubs by being pressed into a softened piece of tool steel. This is then hardened and used to make working dies by the same process, using a press that can exert many tons of pressure to form the design in the working die face. The transfer process is master hub, master die, working hub, working die. The master tools are never used to strike coins.

When the planchets meet the dies, it's in a coin press. This is a machine that is capable of driving one die into the planchet - which is either resting on the opposing die or is being held against it - with lots of pressure. For example, a cent requires about 25 tons per square inch, while the old silver dollars needed

Q: *What is a "device" on a coin?*

A: *A device is the principal element of a design, such as a bust.*

Q: *Why are some coins listed as "with arrows at date," or "without arrows?"*

A: *The arrows were added, especially to the 1853 coins, to signify the reduction in weight resulting from changes in the law affecting the weight. The earlier silver coins contained silver worth more than their face value, so they left circulation rapidly. The new weights were intended to bring the silver content down to match the face value.*

150 tons of pressure per square inch. The planchet is resting on the other die, so when the strike occurs, both sides of the coin are formed at the same time. If the coin has a reeded edge, this is formed at the same time by a collar, often called the third die, which surrounds the planchet and has the reeding cut into the inside edge of the collar.

A very popular misconception is that the obverse and reverse are struck separately, along with the collar. Remember what you learned in physics class in school and you will realize that the principal of equal and opposite forces applies to striking a coin. The strike forms both sides and the edge of the coin in one stroke, or two or more for proof coins.

Lots of things can happen in the coin-making process, including many things that quality control doesn't want to happen. You'll find a chapter on Minting Varieties later on in the book.

One more important point to make is that most mints use the same equipment, often from the same manufacturer, so something that happens to a U.S. coin can usually be found duplicated on a coin from another country. That, too, will be discussed in the chapter on World Coins.

Q: *Why are U.S. coin measurements given in millimeters when we are all used to inches?*

A: *There is a very logical reason for using millimeters, as they are parts of a meter, and the meter is the official standard of measurement of the U.S. government. Despite the reluctance of Congress and the public to follow through, the U.S. has been officially on the metric standard since 1883 when the National Bureau of Standards declared the meter the official standard for all government transactions. At that time the inch was officially defined as being 25.4005 millimeters. Stick to inches if you wish, but the decimal-based metric system is far more accurate and easy to use. One example: The English inch is a different length than our inch; it is actually 0.00012 mm longer.*

Chapter 2

HOW DO I START?

Getting started is the easy part. Take a look at the change in your pocket. You may well find a coin that attracts your interest enough for a closer look. No doubt there's a state quarter or two in there. Granted, it's much more difficult today than it was back in the 1960s when silver coins, Buffalo nickels and even Indian Head cents could turn up in your pocket. Admittedly, pocket change isn't what it used to be. However, with the State quarters coming along at regular intervals and the Lewis and Clark nickels, things are looking up for that pocket-change collection.

Do you know the difference between a coin, a medal or a token?

The 1937 buffalo nickel

Coins

Tokens

Medals

Most people don't and the result is that all three get labeled as coins. There are very distinct differences, as shown by the definitions. Please jump ahead to the glossary and read the three definitions. You will come away with a much better understanding of what a coin is and how it differs from a medal or a token. As you collect, apply those definitions. Already you have learned three key facts.

The next step is to visit your local library and sit down with one of their reference books or price guides for coins. Leafing through, you will see dozens of different coins, even in the same denomination. Chances are that at least one will catch your eye - especially gold.

Remember my advice, "Walk before you run"? Put your checkbook out of reach and keep looking. A first big mistake here can do permanent damage to your finances. If you want to collect, find something to start with that is common enough to be easily affordable.

For many years, cent collectors far outnumbered those collecting other denominations. Today, the State quarters are at the top of the list, followed by silver dollars, with cents coming in third or fourth. This should not stop you if you decide to collect cents. Actually, at the risk of not heeding my own advice, I can recommend cents as a good place to start. Get yourself a folder or album and see what you can do about filling the holes. If you make mistakes here, the losses will be minimal compared to more expensive series.

The State quarters are another good place to start. If you already have several states represented in the coffee mug or tray where they are accumulating, then you are ready to make them into a collection. A local coin shop or a bookstore will have folders or albums that you can buy, which have holes for both the Philadelphia and Denver issues (See the State Quarter chapter).

A collector using a hand lens to look at a coin.

Learn by looking. When you look at a coin, what's the first thing you check?

Usually it's the date. To go on from there, develop a routine that you use for every coin It goes something like this:

Pick up the coin. Look at the date, then the mintmark. Look at all the elements of the obverse design. Then turn the coin over and look at all the elements of the reverse design. Look for obvious damage and telltale signs that the coin has been whizzed or cleaned. Check the edge for problems. Then, on to the next coin. Don't break your routine unless there is something highly unusual that you've spotted.

Popular coin magnifier

Another important rule - don't depend on the unaided eye to see everything on your coin. Use a low-power magnifier (3-5X) for large numbers of coins with a 15 to 20X lens for a close-up look at some small detail on the coins. This strength will catch doctoring or cleaning.

This takes time, but as you gain experience, you will be able to speed up the process. Veteran collectors can readily spot problems at a glance. You too can have a photographic memory, but it takes practice. The more coins you look at - following your routine - the quicker you will imprint the design in your memory and can quickly spot anything that's "wrong" with the coin, whether it's a die defect, a striking problem or damage before or after the strike. Above all, resist the urge to glance at the date and go on to the next coin.

As you start out, especially if you are looking for minting varieties, you will quickly start a pile of coins with something "different." As you gain knowledge, go back through the pile. There will be several coins that puzzle you. You can't remember why you set them back. There will be others that you have learned are damaged or for some other reason need to go back into circulation. This is all part of the learning process.

You'll probably quickly exhaust your resources, especially your pocket change. The next step is to start looking outside your family circle. The church collection plates used to be a good source for change to look through, but today most of the donations are checks or paper money. If you have connections at City Hall, the money taken in by parking meters can be a rich supply source.

If you have an account at a local bank, this is a prime place to cultivate the source. Banks have rolls or even bags of coins, but even this source can dry up unless you are willing to pay shipping expenses. You may also find that several bank employees have learned the value of collecting, drying up yet another source.

When you do find a bank willing to sell you coins, you need to learn their policies on returns and stick to following their instructions exactly. Many banks require that you write your name, and sometimes your address or phone number, on the rolls before returning them. Others may open the rolls and count the coins, guarding against rolls filled with washers, a stunt that can get you in big trouble.

If there's a jukebox operator nearby, the odds are that they have a bin full of foreign coins that patrons have used. Some amazing finds can occur as you sort through them. A good source for quarters is any casino that is nearby. Casinos are always willing to sell you rolls - if you're old enough to gamble.

As I urge in a later chapter, join a local coin club. This can lead to coins that you can swap with other members or that you can bid on during the club auctions.

Before you start buying coins to fill the album holes, here's another repeatable piece of advice: "Buy the book before you buy or sell the coin." More on this later. One of my standards that goes with this is: "Know more about the coin than does the person selling it to you." That's going to be tough if your only contacts are veteran coin dealers or collectors, but it's very pertinent advice and a goal to strive for. It will pay you back many times over.

Many collections start with the death of a relative who leaves behind coins, whether an accumulation or a full-blown collection. Few heirs know what to do, so they panic or allow greed to take over and sell out, often reaping only cents on the dollar of actual value. The rule here is patience. Above all, don't be afraid to ask for advice on what to do with the coins. If they are obviously high-value gold coins, for example, you might want to talk to an auction house that specializes in coins.

My standard advice to heirs and to collectors is to first make a list. Put down the denomination, date and mintmark for each individual coin and list by the roll if they are wrapped and marked.

The coins are not going to lose value as long as they are properly stored, so learn enough about them so that you can decide whether to sell or whether to continue where the collection left off. Over the long term, almost any grouping of coins, especially an established collection, is going to increase in value.

Don't buy out the store. Add to your collection slowly, savoring each new addition. Don't be a checkbook collector. Study each coin you want to buy. Research it. Learn to grade it yourself and compare your grading with the dealer's marking. Assert your pride of ownership, but don't broadcast the fact that you are a coin collector. Burglars assume that anyone with two coins to rub together is rich in potential loot.

Learning the basics of handling your coins is important enough to warrant a chapter on the topic. Read it before you touch any uncirculated or proof coin.

If you've already got a collection started, I recommend that you read the rest of this book before continuing your collection, as there is a lot of valuable information that can save you a lot of problems. If you haven't yet gotten past the accumulation stage, it wouldn't hurt to read the whole book before you start. I'll guarantee you'll learn some new information.

Chapter 3

HOW TO HANDLE YOUR COINS

Ever seen a grown man cry? You will, if you mishandle one of his collectible coins. That's a lesson that you need to learn quickly and take to heart. Despite the fact that (most) coins are metal, their surfaces are extremely fragile. A dropped coin is a damaged coin, with a corresponding sharp drop in collector value.

Right along with the advice of "Don't clean your coins" is "Don't touch your coins." Obviously, that's a bit extreme, but it's a clear warning that you need to know how to work with your collection without damaging your coins.

Rule No. 1 - Always pick up and hold your coins by the edge, never by the faces. If you are working

Always hold a coin by the edges to prevent fingerprints from being permanently etched onto the coin surface.

with upper-grade, uncirculated or proof coins, a pair of lintless cotton gloves are strongly recommended. Latex or plastic gloves are not recommended because they often have powder or lubricants on them that could potentially harm your coins.

Why shouldn't you touch your coins? Because the human skin contains acids that will etch a fingerprint into the surface of a coin in a matter of a few minutes. Once that etching occurs, there is no way to remove it without doing permanent damage to the coin and to its collecting value.

In the chapter on Security and Storage, I make the point that you need to protect your collection from well-meaning, but ignorant friends or relatives that want to touch. You can warn all you want, but the natural urge is to "feel" and the result will be permanent fingerprints or more damage if a coin is accidentally dropped. A good rule is to never take a coin out of its holder when showing it to someone - unless they happen to be a fellow collector you can trust to handle the coin properly.

If you have a well-worn coin, or a copper or copper alloy coin that has darkened considerably, then you don't need to be as careful, but it's better to make a habit of treating all your coins as valuable collectibles and giving them care.

Many an old-time collector or dealer will use the "ring" test to determine if a coin is silver. Unfortunately, besides being a negative test, it potentially damages the coin, since it involves dropping the coin on a hard surface. It's a negative test, because the slightest fissure or internal crack in the coin will make it sound like a lead washer. A scale will tell you as much or more about your coin and its use is a non-destructive test. Don't let someone else "ring" your coin, either.

To make a point, never cut, scratch, polish, rub or otherwise damage a coin in an attempt to determine the metal content. As one example, it is virtually impossible to cut through copper plating on a coin, as it curls around the sharp edge. You'd have to cut the coin in half to see what the core metal is. Every cut, scratch, polish mark or rub is going to cut any collector value in half or worse.

Never allow anyone else to perform these acts on your coin, either. They should know better by now, but there are still collectors and dealers who reach for a knife whenever there is a question about metal content. As with the ring test, a safe, non-destructive test can be performed with a scale.

You will hear a lot about "mint surface" or "mint-produced surface." That's the catchword for today's collectors. The surface appearance of the coin that is imparted by the minting process is what makes a coin so fragile. Damage or destroy that surface and you have seriously damaged or destroyed the coin's collector value. The whole theory of collecting coins revolves around protecting and preserving that mint surface.

In the next chapter, you will read about the pitfalls of cleaning your coins. It explains details that even veteran collectors misunderstand. As you gain experience, you will see for yourself why we make such a big issue of handling your coins with care.

Chapter 4

DESTRUCTIVE AND NON-DESTRUCTIVE CLEANING

This is a good place to repeat, "Don't clean your coins." If you don't learn anything else from this book, just that maxim is worth the price of admission.

Destructive cleaning will reduce the collector value as much as 50 percent or even more. Unless you are an expert at cleaning, almost anything you do is going to cut the value. This was not always the case. Back in the 1970s, experts recommended cleaning. Today, these same experts will refuse to handle a cleaned coin.

The typical response from people who don't take advice kindly is, "I'll do as I please with my coins and you can go jump in the lake!" If you are one of those, then don't waste time reading any further, but your heirs will not appreciate your independence.

I know of one collector who had thousands of silver dollars. Every one had been harshly cleaned with Bon Ami and every new coin he bought got the same treatment, despite dire warnings from friends and dealers he did business with. The result - the only value left was the silver content, less than an ounce in each coin.

A second collector put his coins through a rock tumbler, ruining the collector value. I had the task

Q: *I've got a lot of coins that I found with a metal detector that I expect to sell to collectors. How do I go about cleaning them?*

A: *I just got off the phone with someone who had found a potentially valuable coin and promptly used a pencil eraser to clean it up to be able to read the date and inscription. My unpleasant duty was to have to tell the finder that the coin's value had automatically been cut in half. Removing accumulated dirt and grease is all right, just so long as you don't use any abrasive, abrasive cleaner or acid based cleaner.*

Most non-collectors don't stop to consider that if a coin is badly corroded, covered with a thick coating of oxides, etc., that it has no special value to a collector, regardless of how much you "pretty" it up. It's still a badly pitted, corroded coin with little or no numismatic value. The most valuable coin in the world would be nearly worthless in such condition.

of telling him his coins were worthless to collectors after he flew to where I lived to show them to me.

There's a second group that reacts to this advice by bringing up dozens of "tried and true" cleaning methods that "really work," which they use as an excuse to ignore advice.

But, they have a point. There are certain methods involving the use of neutral solvents or other solutions that don't affect the coin metal and won't damage the coin.

The easiest way to explain the difference is to divide cleaning into two categories - destructive and non-destructive. Destructive cleaning includes any abrasive or acid that will attack the coin metal. Non-destructive methods include virtually anything that will dissolve dirt and grease without harming the metal.

Any abrasive is destructive. No matter how fine the abrasive particles, they are going to scratch the surface of the coin. Whether sandpaper, crocus cloth, baking soda or a pencil eraser - to mention just a few - abrasives will damage your coin. It isn't even safe to use a soft cloth or your finger to rub the surface of a coin, because the cloth or finger will pick up fine particles and act just like sandpaper.

A weak solution of soap (not detergent) and distilled water is one example of a non-destructive cleaning method. Even so, this solution can damage proof coins or almost any upper-grade copper or copper-alloy coin that has copper as the major ingredient. For those coins that won't be damaged by it, the next step is a thorough rinse in distilled water and then allowing them to air dry, or pat dry. Remember, no rubbing. Use distilled water, because the chlorine in tap water will discolor your coins.

A word about sonic cleaners that use ultrasound to remove dirt. If properly used, they are safe for most coins. They cannot be safely used on upper-grade or proof coins. For circulated coins, put a single coin in the bowl and clean it. Then dump out the bowl and rinse to remove any grit before putting the next coin in.

Heavily encrusted coins can be soaked for several months in olive oil. The oil won't damage the coin further, but it will eventually dissolve the crust. Trying to restore badly corroded coins is a waste of time. Even if you successfully remove the corrosion, there is permanent damage underneath, leaving you with a near worthless coin. The same applies to the patina on ancient coins.

Acetone is frequently used to clean coins, as it won't attack the metal. However, since it is extremely flammable, it should only be used in a well-ventilated room, or better yet, outdoors. Fingernail polish remover contains acetone and it can be used on worn or darkened coins, but it may contain ingredients that might damage or discolor upper-grade or proof coins.

As you can see, proof and uncirculated coins are a real problem. There is no cleaning method that I can, or would, recommend. You will have to live with the coin or dispose of it and buy a problem-free replacement.

Several brand-name (TarnX, Brasso) cleaning solutions are on the market, touted as ideal for cleaning coins. Unfortunately, every one of them contains an acid that will damage the coin beyond repair. They remove tarnish, but they take the surface

Morgan dollar with uneven and unsightly toning.

metal of the coin right along with it, destroying the mint-produced surface.

Many collectors avoid the tarnish term and instead refer to it as "toning." Some toning is pretty, with a rainbow of colors, but most is dark and ugly. Toning fans will pay a substantial premium for a colorful coin, but this fad may fade away like so many others, so I never recommend paying a premium for toning. Adding to the problem, coins can be artificially toned and only an expert can tell the difference. Even they get fooled at times.

Separating destructive from non-destructive cleaning defuses much of the controversy about cleaning, but this is an area where you will be exposed to home remedies of one sort or another almost on a daily basis. Apply the rules that I've laid out here and if you are satisfied, try the method on a low-value coin first before using it on anything in your collection.

Sooner or later you will run into PVC damage, caused by the breakdown of plastic flips or vinyl pages. The first signs are usually a greenish slime. This should be removed immediately, as it indicates that the coin surface is being attacked. You can stop PVC damage, but you can't reverse the damage. See the Security and Storage chapter for more information.

Summing up, not cleaning is the path most collectors should follow. Until and unless you become an expert at cleaning, you are going to do more harm than good. Even the experts have numerous failures for every coin they improve by cleaning. Going a step further, don't buy cleaned coins. There is no way to fully reverse the marks or discoloration left by cleaning, so the coin will not increase in value as well as one that hasn't been cleaned.

Chapter 5

TOOLS YOU NEED

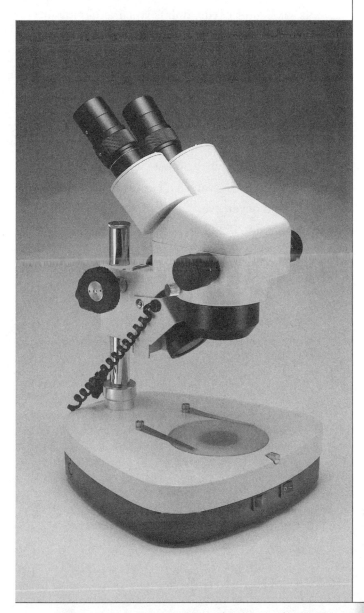

A microscope is a useful tool for the advanced collector.

This chapter will startle a lot of collectors who may think I'm headed for a pick, shovel, chain saw or other tool to use on coins. Those are not the tools a collector needs, unless you are digging up buried treasure, but there are tools that can be of considerable value.

First and foremost, you need something to see with, as I mentioned earlier. Far too many collectors ignore this simple rule, putting their collection in peril to save a couple of dollars. Depending on the unaided eye is by far the most common mistake made by coin collectors at all levels of experience. You should never, ever buy or sell a coin without examining it in detail with a magnifier.

This is not something to skimp on or do without, just to have more to spend on your coins. Don't get by with a low-power magnifier. For active coin collecting, you need at least a 15X or stronger.

A standard 10x magnifier for general identification.

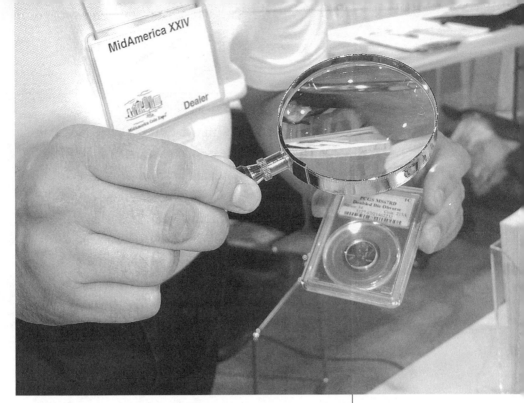

The "X" means "times," so a 15X lens enlarges the image to 15 times normal size. 10X is the minimum standard for most minting varieties. If you can't see it with 10X, then it's not likely to have any collector value.

A hand lens

The lens you use should be tailored to your personal needs. If you look at a lot of coins, by the roll or bag, you should have about a 3X to 5X for general examinations, with a stronger lens for a close-up look at something turned up by the lower-power lens.

When you shop for a magnifier, you will find a wide range of prices. The more expensive ones are likely to have glass lenses, while the cheaper ones depend on plastic lenses. The latter will scratch easily, while the glass will stand up better. I have a 14X glass lens that I bought in 1967 that I've used almost every day since then.

Some come with two or three lenses that can be used separately or in combination to give you different levels of magnification. Try them out and pick the one you are most comfortable with. A lanyard that goes around your neck will keep you from leaving it on the table when you walk away.

One thing you will learn when using a lens is that you will be able to spot coins that have been "doctored" - altered to hide defects. That beautiful, shiny coin that you see will - under a lens - turn out to have been buffed or polished, or even sandblasted - alterations you likely would never catch without the lens.

If your collecting career leads you into research or authentication, or even if you just want to take a detailed look at your coins, a microscope is the next step up. A good stereo with glass lenses will cost you upwards of $250 to $300. It's mandatory that it cover a range from about 20X up to about 40X. The 1200X school microscopes are too powerful for coin work. You will find that with the coin resting on the platform, you can see a lot more than when you are holding the coin in your hand.

When using a strong hand lens or a microscope, turn and tilt the coin to get the light from different angles. This will expose such common problems as light, or reflection doubling, caused by the light bouncing off a shiny coin. It will also help you catch defects, doctoring or maybe even some hub doubling, which in some instances can increase the value of a coin.

I commandeered a plastic cup with a flat bottom from the kitchen and put that on the microscope upside down. The coin goes on the cup and I can turn it in any direction by turning the cup, without touching the coin.

Next in importance after a magnifier is a scale. Just weighing a coin can tell you volumes about it, especially if you get into collecting minting varieties. Routinely weighing coins you purchase or find may help catch some of the counterfeits or save you from buying a fake.

Early in my collecting career, I discovered that a Redding powder scale is ideal for the coin collector. It weighs up to 500 grains, to a tenth of a grain. They are available from gun shops that carry reloading equipment. On today's market, there are digital electronic scales that will fit in your shirt pocket. For really serious work, I have an Ohaus scale that can do specific-gravity tests.

If we consider a computer to be a tool, there is a lot that one can do for the collector. There is a variety of software on the market that will sort out and even evaluate your collection. In a pinch, you can use almost any word processor to log your collection. I've used WordPerfect for more than two decades for that purpose, as the search mode will find anything and everything.

A big item is the storage available, where you can put photos or scans of your coins and keep research material handy. The copying function allows you to copy information to add to your collection.

In the chapter on handling your coins, I didn't mention one tool that can come in handy. It's a pair of plastic tongs. I don't remember just when or where I bought one, but it's been very useful. The spring-loaded jaws have slots that hold the coin so that you don't have to touch it with your fingers.

You will also need a stapler. Again, don't skimp. You need one that will drive the staple through two thicknesses of cardboard. Get one big enough so you can bang on it with your fist. Don't forget my warning about getting too close to the coins with the staples. Don't buy cheap staples, either. They are likely to curl up and die before they make it through the cardboard. I have an old government surplus stapler that has a life expectancy longer than mine. It's big, rugged and won't wear out.

The next item is one you may already have - a pair of needle-nose pliers. These are not to use on the coins, but they do come in handy for your stapling jobs. After you have driven the staples, turn the holder over and flatten the curved ends of the staple right down into the cardboard. Don't do this and sooner or later you will scratch a valuable coin with a staple leg that sticks out. They will also rub on the adjacent coins if you stack them in a box.

An inexpensive protractor will give you an exact reading on a coin struck with a rotated-reverse die. There are also plastic templates that will give you a size reading on a clipped coin. Did I mention that a good light is a must? Some swear by a small halogen light, but for most uses, including photography, a 60- or 100-watt incandescent bulb in a gooseneck or swing-arm lamp will do the trick. Avoid fluorescent lights, as they tend to distort what you see on the coin.

Lastly, a word about metal detectors. I've used them both here in the United States and on beaches in Germany, and I would not recommend them as a collecting tool. The principal reason is that coins left on or in the ground for a lengthy period are usually corroded. The longer they are in the soil, the more corroded they become. If you live in or have access to a desert climate, you may find coins with little or no corrosion, but they would be an exception.

Chapter 6

WHAT'S IT WORTH?

The most common question that I get asked in the mail and on the Internet is one that I can't answer: "What's it worth?" But, nobody else can answer it, either.

Well, why not? The problem is that coin value is not fixed. Since it's not the only item that doesn't have a fixed value, I point out that a coin, just like a house or a car, has to be seen in order to accurately determine the value. The collector value of a coin is the amount over and above the face value that a collector might reasonably be expected to pay for it. It is determined based on a number of factors, the most important being the grade, or exact amount of wear, on a 70-point scale. Other factors include the number minted or the number estimated to survive. Sometimes it even depends on the rarity of a specific grade.

One example of this is the 1931-S cent, the second-lowest mintage Lincoln Wheat cent. Because

1931-S Lincoln Wheat cent

the majority of the coins were saved in uncirculated grades, there is only a $37.50 difference between a coin in Good-4 grade and a MS-60 specimen.

A common request is to provide a price range. That's something I won't do either, because for most people a range is meaningless and perhaps unexpectedly creates a serious problem. As an example, a 1915-D cent is worth $1.50 in the lowest (Good-4) well-worn grade and $1,250 in an uncirculated (MS-65) grade. I give the questioner a range of $1.50 to $1,250.

Automatically he will think, "Then my coin is worth $1,250!" That's human nature. But what comes next is the problem. He goes to a coin dealer and says, "I want to sell my coin." The dealer looks at it and offers a fair price - $12.50, because the coin has wear and would grade about XF-40. The customer cusses him out and leaves, convinced that he was being ripped off. No amount of explaining will change his mind.

As you scout the Internet, you will find helpful people trying to coach someone asking this question by quoting the figures for several different grades. This, sadly, is a waste of time because the person asking the question has no concept of grading and to him, his coin is in "Very Fine" condition.

To the layman, the description is accurate, but condition and grade is not the same thing. His "Very Fine" might be a Good-4 to a numismatist. It doesn't matter if you go into a six-page explanation - the person will go away convinced, because he can see the date and design clearly, that his "Very Fine" condition rates the top grade and quote. Then comes the problem, as noted in the previous paragraph.

The solution is to learn how to grade your coins, a topic covered in the Grading Your Coins chapter. Remember, "Know more about the coin you are buying than does the person selling it." That applies to grading as much, or even more, than other factors.

Then why are there price guides that list several grades and values for each grade? Price guides are just that – guides. To gain the most help from them, you need to know more about coins than the average person. Prices for grades are given, but if you can't grade your coin, how do you know which grade to look at for a value?

You can get by, with only a very basic understanding of the grading system, by settling on an approximate grade and looking that up, but in nearly every case, your guess will be on the high side, even the very high side. At the same time, you could cheat yourself if you take the lowest grade.

As you gain experience, the figures in a price guide will have more meaning for you. However, you need to remember that the prices quoted are retail values, not what a dealer will offer you. While there are price guides with wholesale values, their quotes are an average and most dealers will be using figures above or below the book. You'll find more on that in the Coin Dealers chapter.

A vital point here is that there are two kinds of catalogs, with a lot of confusion about them. A price

Q: *Didn't President Johnson say silver coins would not become scarce?*

A: *In his speech marking the signing of the Coinage Act of 1965, he said: "Some have asked whether silver coins will disappear. The answer is very definitely no. Our present coins won't disappear and they won't even become rarities. If anybody has any idea of hoarding our silver coins, let me say this: Treasury has a lot of silver on hand, and it can be and it will be used to keep the price of silver in line with its value in our present silver coins. There will be no profit in holding them out of circulation for the value of their silver content."*

guide is a reference catalog, not an offer to buy or sell. A catalog that offers coins for sale or offers to buy coins is a sales catalog and the prices quoted are actual sell or buy prices.

Another important point - the figures in any reference catalog, retail or wholesale, are not cast in stone. Dealers use the figures constantly, but they figure their pricing based on a number of other factors. Do not expect to walk into a coin shop and find a coin in the exact grade at the same price as your reference catalog. You might, but the odds are against you.

Telling the two catalogs apart should not be that hard. However, every week or two our editorial staff receives an offer to buy some coin listed in one of our price guides. Every price guide clearly states that it is not a sale catalog and that the publisher does not buy or sell coins. If you are unsure of what a given catalog is, look for an order blank. If you don't find one, you can be reasonably sure it's a reference catalog.

Another misconception about price guides is the conspiracy theory - that they are hiding something or aren't telling the whole story. A typical price guide will have dashes instead of a value for a number of rare coins. Repeatedly, readers will write in asking for the price for that specific coin, ignoring the fact that if a price were available, it would be published.

It's not unusual for a rare coin to not have a value listed. It may have been several decades since the last one appeared in an auction, or any examples were sold privately, with the information never reaching the publisher. Most publishers go to great lengths to eliminate as many of the dashes as possible.

The same thing applies to different designs or series, where you will find "Inc. Above" or "Inc. Below." This simply means that there are no mint records separating two or more designs or series for a given year. The figures are included above or included below in one total. A substantial amount of research has gone into the figures we do have, in a number of cases superseding published figures from the Mint. Veteran researcher Robert W. Julian is responsible for many of the corrected figures gained through months spent in the Library of Congress, going through and cross-checking U.S. Mint records.

The early Mint reports are often incomplete, with figures transposed, faulty arithmetic or other problems. In some instances, the revised figures are based both on uncovered records and a bit of guesswork. They are in general use throughout the hobby, and the several price guides nearly all have the same mintage figures.

Coins tend to gain value over the long haul, if properly stored. In most cases, this gain will be small, but in a few instances there will be a rapid increase, due to a lack of coins to satisfy potential buyers. Many collectors search through quantities of coins, picking out those with more than the usual value, but when they try to sell them, they wonder why nobody wants them.

The misconception here is that just because a coin is listed in a price guide, there is a market for it. The fact is, that since anyone can search coins, there is a surplus of low-value coins, far more than any market for them. Coin values are like any other commodity. If there's a shortage, the price and demand goes up. If there's a surplus, the demand is met and the price goes down.

That's why you will see some fairly recent coins or sets that are listed at prices far above earlier or later dates. It pays to keep a close eye on price changes, because they will tell you when you need to sell or buy for your collection. They will also give you a sense of accomplishment if you already have the "jumpers" in your collection.

Chapter 7

COINS AND THE LAW

The title of this chapter may startle you a bit, but you do have some legal obligations that you should be aware of.

The first and foremost thing that you need to do is to keep a record of all the coins you purchase and all the coins that you sell. This does double duty, as it keeps you informed as to the value of your collection, and obviously an inventory is going to be of major help in planning your collection.

There is software on the market - assuming that you have a computer - that will take care of listing your coins. You can do well using your word processor, which allows you to set up dates and mints with room for varieties or other additions, or extra columns to handle multiple coins.

The second reason is that the IRS requires records to support purchases and sales. If you can't prove what you paid for a given coin that you sell, they can assess any amount above the face value as profit. If you received coins as a gift, it's a good idea to establish a value at the time you received them by going back into price guides for the period. The sooner you start, the fewer problems you will have in finding price records. The better your records, the less likely you are to get audited. This applies to other collectibles, as well. In some instances, the IRS may

Q: *I'm involved in a serious argument. Can private mints issue coins?*

A: *A private mint can mint coins, but a government has to issue the coins. This is a point that many collectors overlook. Even an official mint, such as the U.S. Mint, cannot issue coins. They are a manufacturing facility and they turn the coins over to the Federal Reserve Bank, which has the authority to issue them. Thus, a coin is not legally a coin until the Mint has transferred it to the Federal Reserve Bank for issue. This raises a curious legal question as to how proof and commemorative coins struck and sold directly by the Mint become legal coins.*

require an appraisal by a recognized appraiser.

The third reason is that without an inventory, your heirs or the executor of your estate will have no clue as to what the coins are and what they are worth. In numerous cases, estate coins are sold for a fraction of their actual value because of this lack of knowledge. Leave specific instructions as to how to dispose of the coins in the collection in your will. This is especially true for minting varieties, which require a specialist dealer to handle them.

Very important - if you have a specialty collection, whether minting varieties, Roman coins or tokens, make sure that your list includes the name and contact information for one or more dealers in that specialty. It's not a bad idea to make advance arrangements with your dealer of choice, so that they will be aware of what's coming and will be prepared to follow your wishes.

It's also an excellent idea to make a specific bequest of your collection, either to your estate if there isn't an individual heir who would like to continue it, or to some group that would give your estate a tax benefit, such as the American Numismatic Association in Colorado Springs, Colorado. It is usually a bad idea to bequeath a collection to several non-collectors, which mandates a sale to divide the assets. One of the most common complaints I get from collectors is that there is nobody else in the family who has the slightest interest in coin collecting.

For detailed information and information about state laws affecting your collection, it would be a good idea to contact the IRS for information and your state tax authorities, as well as a tax preparer or CPA. The sale of a major collection can have serious tax liabilities.

Make that resolution right now: "I will keep records for all my collection."

Despite strict Federal laws, you will find counterfeits, altered coins and reproductions freely offered, especially in on-line auctions. The law is clear - mere possession (let alone buying or selling) of counterfeit U.S. and foreign coins is breaking the law. Altered coins also violate the law in most cases and reproductions require the word "COPY" stamped into the metal if they were made after 1975. When you see "COPY" you'll know that the item is worthless to collectors. You will see other collectors and dealers who flout the law with their collections, but this is not a role model to follow.

Just don't get into an argument with them about the legality of their collection. Chances are it will be akin to grabbing a rattlesnake in each hand, as they will defend to the death their "right" to collect fake coins. Of course, ignorance of the law plays a part in some cases. It's not a defense if you get dragged into court.

Q: *Only one of my relatives is interested in coins, so I want him to have my collection after I die. Is there some way I can ensure he will get it?*

A: *Unless you make a will specifically naming him, you may run into problems, or you can give him your collection before you die. The laws vary from state to state so consult a lawyer right away for competent advice on how best to handle the matter. Under IRS regulations, if the collection is worth less than $10,000 it meets the requirements of a gift and need not be reported. If over $10,000, the excess will reduce the estate exempted from tax when you die.*

Chapter 8

AUCTIONS OF ALL KINDS

One of the most popular methods of selling coins is by public auction. There are a small number of auction houses that specialize in numismatic material. In addition, practically every country auction has a selection of coins. More and more business is going to the online auctions on the Internet. Some of these sales are beneficial, but some of them can turn into a headache, especially if you are buying, rather than selling.

A typical coin auction by a coin auctioneer may contain several hundred to several thousand items. Frequently the auction is "named" to recognize the collector who assembled the collection being sold, but many times coins from other consignors are added to the sale.

Expect to pay for the privilege of having your coins auctioned, and expect to pay for the privilege of buying coins in a regular auction, as the current trend is to charge both the seller and the buyer a fee based on the actual sale or "hammer" price. These fees add up to a significant discount in the value of the coins being sold, so it's necessary to consider them when you plan to sell or buy.

There are two general types of auctions, public and private. Obviously, the latter is by invitation only, so unless you are what Las Vegas describes as a "whale," you may not even hear about a private sale.

At a public auction, bidding is usually based on a reserve, or amount that the seller determines is the minimum acceptable bid. If the reserve isn't met, the item is sold back to the consignor.

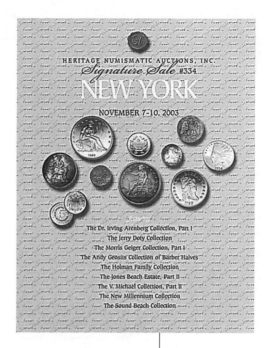

HERITAGE NUMISMATIC AUCTIONS, INC.
Signature Sale #334
NEW YORK
NOVEMBER 7-10, 2003

The Dr. Irving Arenberg Collection, Part I
The Jerry Doty Collection
The Morris Geiger Collection, Part I
The Andy Geosits Collection of Barber Halves
The Holman Family Collection
The Jones Beach Estate, Part II
The V. Michael Collection, Part II
The New Millennium Collection
The Sound Beach Collection

Rare coin auction catalog.

Bidding may involve people in the auction room, on the telephone or increasingly on the Internet, or who have submitted written bids by mail, called "The Book," so if you are attempting to follow the bidding, you will find it isn't easy. Book bidders usually offer a range, giving the auctioneer discretion to continue bidding, stopping when the bid level exceeds the range.

Major auction sales feature catalogs, listing every lot and providing photos of the actual coins. In many cases, especially with a very valuable coin, the cataloger goes to great lengths to provide as much information about the coin as possible, especially if it comes out of a "name" collection. Thus, coin catalogs become important reference material for your library. It's virtually impossible to read through an auction catalog without learning several things you didn't already know.

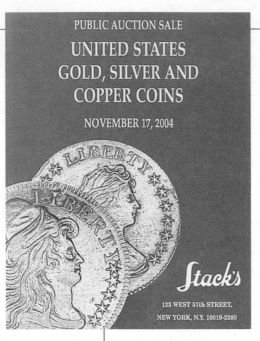

PUBLIC AUCTION SALE

UNITED STATES
GOLD, SILVER AND
COPPER COINS

NOVEMBER 17, 2004

Stack's

123 WEST 57th STREET,
NEW YORK, N.Y. 10019-2280

Auction catalog

Collecting these catalogs is an interesting sidelight to coin collecting. The catalogs are sold by the auction houses in order to defray the cost of printing them. For a really major sale, the auctioneer may have special (free) catalogs made up for big bidders, some even bound in leather. Eventually, the excess catalogs wind up in the hands of a numismatic book dealer, where groups of catalogs are divided into lots and sold.

The Internet is playing more and more of a role, with photos of the lots usually posted on the auction house's Web site. The potential buyer thus has the tools on his computer, such as Photoshop, to copy, magnify or enlarge photos to suit his needs. A growing number of bidders either submit bids by computer or by telephone. A firm or two actually conduct their sales exclusively on the telephone, but the big trend these days is the on-line auction. There are several firms offering on-line auctions, the largest being eBay.

The problem for the average potential bidder is that these are "sight unseen" auctions, with very limited regulation. This means you bid at your own risk for something you haven't had a chance to examine. Pictures, if provided, often are hazy or out of focus and, in extreme cases, may not even be of the coin being offered. The hobby auction houses make a point of illustrating their catalogs with actual photographs of the coins being offered.

For most collectors, buying sight unseen is so potentially hazardous that I recommend that you never buy a coin without examining it, at least until you can readily do your own grading. (See the next chapter, TV or not TV, for similar problems.) As noted for country auctions, these Internet sales are a bonanza for sellers. As always, read the rules.

Hobby auction houses have standard rules, many of them the same or similar across the industry. They cover usual bidding rules, procedure for a claim, payment arrangements and other housekeeping. Above all, if you plan to participate in an auction, read the rules carefully. They are usually posted at the very beginning of the auction catalog. Catalogs are usually sent out a month or two before the sale, so you have plenty of time to study the information. Knowing the rules going in may save you a goodly sum of money and will help you avoid the humiliation of making a challenge, only to find that it was covered in the rules.

Note that an auction lot may consist of one coin, or it may contain several hundred or more. One universal rule in coin auctions is that you can't bid on a single coin included in a multiple group, you have to bid on the lot. The description will include the number of coins in any multiple lot.

All of the major auction houses provide an opportunity to examine the lots prior to the sale. Auctions held in conjunction with a coin show usually have a room where potential customers can request an opportunity to examine any of the lots. As I mentioned before, there is a lot to learn from catalogs. Learn by doing. Examine some of the lots and compare them closely with the catalog descriptions. Looking at the coin, you can see whether your grading matches with the experts.

The auctioneers are always on the lookout for scam artists attempting to buck the system. "Ringing" a sale, an outlawed method where a group of bidders who agree not to bid against each other and then divide up the spoils, is one that you won't see, nor will you see a "Buy" bid that has an unlimited ceiling. Two or more "buy" bidders in the same sale could result in chaos. The auction houses pride themselves on running auctions that are fair to everyone participating. Note that this is a different meaning for "ringing" from that used in Chapter 3, referring to a "ring" test.

Country auctions are a terrific method to dispose

of low- to medium-value coins, for the seller. For the buyer, it's a can of worms. You need only to attend one or two such auctions to realize that most of the coins are selling for two or three times their actual value and silver dollars are likely to bring even more. Rare is the auctioneer who knows coins well enough to do a credible selling job. The odds are that the coins will be mishandled and improperly stored. High-value coins should be reserved for a regular coin auction.

Many local clubs hold auctions as a part of their meetings or schedule periodic mail-bid auctions. See the chapter on joining a club for additional information. There are other forms of auctions - silent auctions, Dutch auctions and others - but you will rarely run into one involving coins, unless it is a charity auction that takes donations of coins.

Know the rules, pay close attention to what's going on and make it a rule not to bid on something that you haven't examined or researched. Prepare for an auction by looking at the lots and checking them against a current price guide so that you can plan your bidding strategy. Don't forget that cardinal rule for any auction, "Know more about the coin than does the person selling it to you."

The opposite of an auction is a private treaty sale. This refers to a one-on-one sale where two people buy, sell or trade coins with each other. Since a sale by a dealer to a customer is a private treaty sale, they far outnumber auctions. Literally it means to come to an agreement on price.

Chapter 9

TV OR NOT TV, HOTEL ROOMS AND NEWSPAPERS

Here I'm going to quote a rule and then explain why. "If the company doesn't advertise in the hobby press, then run - don't walk - for the nearest exit."

Everyone with cable TV has seen them. They are the pitchmen who tout coins with "facts" and hype in a double-talk mixture that can even confuse the experts. What they are selling is often overgraded and usually grossly overpriced. That isn't illegal, but it can do serious damage to your checkbook. All you need to do is to visit a local coin dealer and the odds are that you can save as much as 50 percent, perhaps even more, depending on the particular coin.

Beware of telemarketers. Make it a rule never to buy from someone who calls you out of the blue, which is known in the industry as a "cold call." Either hang up or demand that they mail you literature about their offer. If you are already on a sucker list, contact the proper agency and get your phone number(s) put on the national "Do Not Call" list. List your cell phone at the same time.

The third group to avoid is the salespeople who want to sell you various commemoratives, colorized coins, plated coins, miniature coins and other questionable pieces. There are two key things to look for that will tell you that there's mischief afoot.

Custom-minted medal for the American Numismatic Association's National Summer Convention.

One is if they misuse the word "coin" to cover privately issued medals, as for example to refer to a "commemorative coin" that they have had struck privately. While there are legal commemorative coins issued by several governments, most of the offers fall into the private-medal category. Several sports memorabilia companies commonly run ads referring to their player medals as "coins."

The second thing to look for is a name somewhat similar to the U.S. Mint, or that sounds official, but is accompanied by a disclaimer that the company is not affiliated with the U.S. Mint. There are numerous variations of this theme, so your best bet is to stick to recognized collectibles.

Read the fine print. If there is something you don't understand, find out what it means. Often the language or terms are intentionally and deliberately confusing. A typical ad may offer what seems to be a gold or silver piece, when actually it has only a very thin plating of bullion over base metal. For example, "layered" refers to a very thin plating, not a solid-bullion coin. It's a jewelry term appropriated to medals to confuse the reader.

For many years, it was illegal to gold-plate U.S. coins. When that restriction was lifted, it gave the hucksters an opportunity to flood the market with plated coins. It's important to know that the gold plating is so thin that it contains only a few cents worth of gold, worth only a small fraction of the cost of recovering it from the coin. The result is an altered coin, with no collector value and one that will never appreciate like a normal coin. Read the fine print and then run.

Legal coins that have been altered by adding colored enamel after they leave the mint are just that - altered coins. This means they probably will never surface on the price charts, nor will other similar alterations. Collectors don't want them, so there is little or no aftermarket for them. One or two of the government mints, such as the Royal Canadian Mint, offer mint-produced colored coins that are legitimate collectibles.

Ads for dubious collectibles also appear in newspapers and magazines, especially service-group publications. Full-color, full-page ads cost a

United States 20th Century type coin set in frame.

substantial amount, so you can be sure the profit margin is tremendous.

Also appearing in newspapers are ads directly aimed at the proverbial "little old ladies in tennis shoes." One glance and you recognize the pitch line, "We pay up to XXX for certain coins." They hole up in a hotel or motel room and willing victims crowd in to sell their coins (and jewelry and watches) for a fraction of their real value. Several years ago, I fielded a complaint that a woman wound up selling several gold coins for face value to one of these motel buyers.

As you gain experience, you will realize that all of these ads are based on the lack of knowledge shown by the general public. These companies deliberately target the uninformed and they find dupes by the thousands. One of the common victims is a relative or friend of a collector. When birthday or Christmastime comes around they are looking for an appropriate gift. More often than not, they present the collector with coins purchased from one of these sources.

A good friend of mine, a longtime collector, took me into his confidence. He showed me a Christmas present his son and daughter had given him. It was a type set of U.S. coins in a frame, under glass. In most instances a nice gift. In this case, every coin in the case had been heavily cleaned, obvious to the unaided eye. My friend was too much of a gentleman to point out the error of their choice, but every time he sees that set he will remember that his children got ripped off.

That's why I recommend the hobby press. Contrary to the "we'll take anything" attitude of the newspapers and magazines, the hobby press refuses most such advertising and in the event of complaints, will cancel the rest. They have consumer advocates on staff to resolve complaints. I work for the hobby press, but I'm giving you an unbiased recommendation here. I've seen virtually every scam and shady deal that has come along in the last 37 years and I've seen readers who got seriously hurt by buying into non-hobby offers.

Rather than falling for the here-today-gone-tomorrow ads, patronize your local coin dealers. Like any other businessman, they are going to be here next week, next month and probably years to come. See the chapter on Coin Dealers for more information.

Chapter 10

SECURITY AND STORAGE

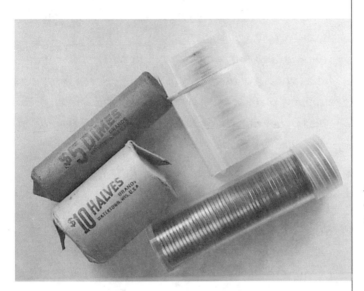

Assortment of coin storage rolls.

Security means many things to a coin. It means being safe from thieves, from fire, floods, mishandling - even from pets. Security comes in several levels, the key determination usually being the overall value of the collection.

Storage ties right in with security, because a major point of storage is that it be in a safe place, not just from fire and flood, but also from contamination in the air and protection from physical damage from rubbing or banging into other coins.

Typically, the average coin collection winds up in one of several places - under the bed, on a closet shelf or back in a lower corner, in the basement, or

Q: *Is Mylar "always" safe for coins?*

A: *Pure Mylar is safe, but if it contains any impurities it may cause problems. Also, because it is very brittle, it should never be used for shipping coins through the mail. I've seen dozens of coins that have split out of their flips in transit, or even just by dropping them in the flip. Mylar also will scratch coins if they moved about frequently within the flip. Many dealers still use flips with PVC for temporary storage or mailing, so if you buy coins that come in flips, remove them at once unless the flips are Mylar. If this is all you have, reinforce all four sides with tape before shipping coins. It's best when shipping one or two large coins to tape the flip, holder or envelope to a thin piece of cardboard, and even better to run tape on all four sides of the holder.*

the attic. That's at least until it gets so large that it gets moved to the garage or even a shed or other outbuilding.

These locations can be readily summed up - bad and worse.

Under the bed is fine (except for the dust) for all those cents you collected over the years and the rolls of nickels, but the silver dimes, quarters and halves will surprise you if you add up the silver value. Besides, there are the three $20 gold pieces that Aunt Hattie left you in her will. More on Aunt Hattie in a minute.

A closet shelf will take only so much weight and nothing will age you like waking up to the crash of the box to the floor. Any place in the closet is fine for small quantities of low-value coins, but save the heavy and expensive coins for better accommodations.

Basements are just plain bad. Too damp. Coins corrode. End of story.

Attics are also bad because they're too hot. Coins, despite being solid metal in most cases, like human conditions. Moderate humidity, moderate heat and your coins are as happy as you are. High heat speeds the deterioration of almost any storage media and is a key factor in damage incurred from plastic holders containing PVC. An important point is to not only dispose of plastic flips that contain PVC, but get rid of the plastic-vinyl album pages that contain the chemical. Fumes from PVC will seep into your neutral plastic holders stored in a PVC-laced vinyl page.

All of the above are the first places, along with the freezer in the garage, that burglars will search for valuables. Keep your high-value coins in the bank.

Home safes are costly and potentially hazardous to your coins. A safe that protects from fire has liquid in the lining that can damage your coins. A safe that protects from burglars won't protect the contents from fire for more than a few minutes. Have a heart-to-heart talk with the safe salesman before buying one.

A small safe

Aunt Hattie's stash of valuable gold coins.

A bank box is expensive but it will protect from some - but not all - hazards. More fine print to read. Your collection insurance will cover coins in the bank, probably at a lower rate than those kept at home. Do not depend on the bank's insurance, which may have significant gaps. This is where Aunt Hattie's gold coins belong, along with any other high-value pieces you have. Talk to your insurance agent. A homeowner's or renter's policy will not cover a coin collection in most cases; it will require additional coverage.

Custom coin storage containers

To protect coins from themselves, you need to do several things. First, pick an arbitrary number, say $100. Sort your collection and separate out the expensive coins. Depending on your collection, you may want to lower the dividing line to $50.

The expensive coins will need individual inert hard plastic holders. If they have already been sealed (slabbed) in a plastic holder by a grading service, it will save you having to do it. The hard plastic holders are expensive, but they will pay for themselves many times over by protecting the value of the coins they contain.

The bulk coins can go into inert plastic coin tubes. Be careful and slide the coins in, rather than dropping them on top of each other.

Some of your coins may be in plastic flips or 2x2 cardboard holders. First separate and replace any plastic flips that are soft and flexible, as they contain PVC that can do permanent damage to your coins or paper money. Replace them with the stiff Mylar flips that are free of PVC.

The Mylar flips can also damage your coins if you move the coin in and out frequently. If you need to take the coin out on a regular basis, it's time to upgrade to a cardboard holder or a hard plastic holder.

Standard cardboard coin album, recommended for short-term storage only.

The cardboard holders have a Mylar window so you can see the faces of the coin easily. They need to be stapled together so follow closely. The usual procedure is to put a staple in each of the three open sides after you fold the holder over the coin. The most common mistake in the hobby is to put the staples as close to the coin as possible. This risks a slip and a staple jammed into the coin, or the overhang at the tip of the stapler will bang down on the coin and damage it. Either way you've lowered the value of your coin by half or more. Cardboard holders should not be used for long-term storage - more than six months.

Here's the relative order of common storage media from best to worse:

1. *Inert hard plastic holders, new coin albums*

2. *Inert hard plastic coin tubes*

3. *2x2 cardboard holders*

4. *Mylar flips*

5. *Paper or plastic rolls*

6. *Old albums and coin boards*

7. *Canvas mint bags or aluminum foil*

Old style plastic coin storage tubes.

Bank-wrapped rolls in paper offer no protection from contamination and very little protection from physical contact. The plastic used in bank wrapped rolls apparently contains PVC and are open at the ends to contamination. Coin boards require handling of the coins to fill them and the coins are exposed to all forms of damage. The old albums rank with coin boards. New ones fitted for slabbed coins or for other hard-plastic holders would rank at the top of the list.

The worst possible storage media are the canvas mint bags. The coins are loose, so they scrape against each other every time the bag is moved. If the bag is thrown or dropped, the damage is immensely worse. See the chapter on Home Remedies for additional storage information.

Canvas bags of coins.

A fad that you will run into sooner or later are the premiums offered for "mint packaging" or "unopened rolls." Both can cost you money. An unopened roll is almost guaranteed to deteriorate faster than one kept in a coin tube. Several years ago, Japan issued coin sets in plastic that contained PVC. The set price was quite high, but once the coins had been removed and safely stored, there was no way to prove they came from a set. You can easily run into a similar catch-22 situation if you follow the fads.

One storage medium that you want to avoid at all costs is aluminum foil, which is actually worse than a canvas bag. Despite being recommended by at least one author, the foil in contact with other metals will corrode them as soon as any moisture enters the picture. I once dug up some rolls of silver dollars that had been buried in the sandy floor of a garage with a leaky roof. Every one of the coins was corroded, ruining any collector value they might have had.

A key problem with proof and uncirculated coins is that they may discolor or tone in your hard-plastic holders. While a defective holder might be at fault, it's much more likely that the coin was exposed to contamination in the mint, long before you got it. I've seen fingerprints turn up on properly stored coins, invisible until they aged.

A key part of security is keeping mum about the fact you are a collector. Sure, you want to display your coins for your friends and relatives, but a casual remark by one of them could be overheard and lead burglars right to your house. Impress on everyone who knows you collect that they are not to mention your collecting interests under any circumstances.

Lincoln cents severely damaged from corrosion.

Chapter 11

HOME REMEDIES

Some of the first people you are likely to run into in the hobby are throwbacks to the old snake-oil salesmen. Beware of their potions and remedies!

The rule for this chapter is: "Stick to products intended for and tested for coins." This applies especially to products seen on TV that magically remove tarnish from a coin, or other similar products, all of which will do permanent damage to your coins.

Remember, "Don't clean your coins." Earlier I mentioned a couple of metal cleaners that you don't want near your coins. The same thing is true of the numerous home remedies that collectors come up with. Coca Cola is a great cleaner for your windshield, but don't use it on coins. It has acids that will do permanent damage. If you missed the chapter on cleaning coins, go back and read it.

You need to break yourself of being cheap. Don't use products intended for other purposes for coin storage. Glass pill bottles make great coin containers, until you drop one. You'll be picking glass out of the carpet for months.

Paper, tissue paper, cardboard and envelopes are bad medicine for coins. They contain sulfur, which immediately goes to work to turn your coins black. That rules out the shoebox as well. The 2x2 paper

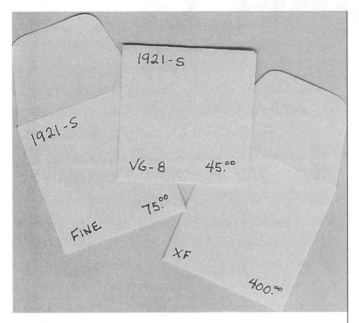

2 x 2 paper coin storage envelopes.

coin envelopes are made with paper free of sulfur and are safe to use for a limited time. Many non-collectors pack their coins in cotton fibers or cotton-lined envelopes. This, too, is bad for the health of the coins because there is no protection from contaminants or liquids in the air.

One notable exception to our rule is plastic food-storage bags. They don't contain PVC, so they are safe to use to store bulk coins, with the notation that loose coins in a bag are going to slide, bump and ding other coins. Contact marks will definitely affect the collector value.

The shoebox can be replaced with a covered plastic bin that provides adequate protection, and can be more easily handled and stored. The tight covers provide important protection from contamination in the air.

Chapter 12

RULES FOR BUYING AND SELLING

Like any other financial transaction, buying and selling coins has some specific rules that you need to be aware of as you start adding to your collection.

One of the most common standards has to do with returning a coin you decide not to buy for any of a number of reasons. The rule here is: "Do not open a sealed holder or stapled 2x2 cardboard holder without the specific written approval and permission of the seller." Opening the holder automatically voids any guarantee and gives the seller legal grounds to refuse to accept the return.

If you stop and think for a moment, this standard is vitally important to both the buyer and the seller. If the holder has been tampered with or opened, there is no proof that the coin inside is the one involved in the transaction. Once the dealer is convinced that it is his coin, the door is open for a replacement to satisfy the customer.

Many collectors worry about having their coins switched by a dealer, but for every dealer who pulls a fast one on a customer there are a hundred or more larcenous souls who will use every trick they know to screw a dealer. Ask any of the dealers you know and they can reel off horror stories for the rest of the day about their problems with customers. You need to realize that fraud is a two-way street.

Don't expect to walk up to a coin dealer and say, "I'm a dealer, so give me a discount." Every dealer has had this happen, so it won't work. You might find a discount under other circumstances, but the first question you would be asked is: "What's your resale number?" Dealers will discount coins to wholesale levels to people they know are dealers, but only very rarely to individuals who are not dealers.

That's not to say that you can't dicker with the dealer to try to get a better price. Depending on the dealer's circumstance, you might get a small discount, especially if you buy several coins. The time of day, the flow of business or a coin that has lain unsold for months can affect a dealer's decision to discount a price.

When you shop for coins, take a want list - with prices - along, so that you can check off the coins you buy. It will help jog your memory and bring you back to reality. Remember, there are no "fire sale" prices for coins. I've seen collectors lugging the telephone-book size *Standard Catalog of World Coins* around a bourse floor, but most depend on the dealer having a price guide to consult.

If you are collecting a series, or a group of coins, it's tempting to buy the less-expensive coins first. The best advice is to do just the opposite. Buy the expensive coins first, as they are the ones most likely to appreciate. If you wait until last, you may find that your key coins have attained unaffordable price tags. But, take time to learn your grading before you start buying big-ticket coins.

Chapter 13

HOW TO ASK QUESTIONS

Would you believe that asking questions is very hard for some people?

Asking questions is something of an art. Many men, as the popular axiom goes, would rather stay lost than ask directions. A lot of questions go unasked because the person is afraid of being laughed at. I don't laugh at or make fun of questions, because how else is the person going to learn?

Those of us who regularly answer questions from collectors have a slogan, "There are no dumb questions." Rather, asking questions is unquestionably the best way to learn. Never be afraid to ask. I am not going to make a joke of your question. Rather I will applaud you for having enough curiosity and interest to go looking for an answer. You will find people who are not professionals deliberately giving misleading or wrong answers on the Internet, treating sincere questions as a big joke. To me this is no joking matter. If you do run into a situation where you suspect an answer, by all means get a second opinion before acting on dubious advice.

When it comes to coins, asking questions is the best way of learning. This is especially true if you have skimped on your reference library. I have a few tips that will make it easier.

When you write or e-mail a question, don't beat about the bush. I have a stack of letters several inches thick that read, "I have a coin (with a die defect). What is it worth?

Describe what you have with plenty - make that all - of the details - size, weight, apparent metal, denomination, date, mintmark and a description of the design. Even if you send a photo or scan, print out all the lettering and numbers on both sides. In other words, include anything that would be helpful to the person answering your question. Ask yourself, "What is wrong with the coin?" Then, answer the question with the best description you can muster.

Photos and scans are another matter. More than 95 percent of them are out of focus so badly that it's hard to even identify the object as a coin. This is useless for identification. A detailed description is often better. But, don't go off the deep end in the opposite direction. Don't go to the expense and delay of having a professional photographer take photos of the coin. Only a handful of photographers have the equipment and knowledge needed to properly photograph a coin.

Coin rubbing created with a sheet of white paper and a pencil.

Wait until your description has been assessed. If the coin is a new variety, I can photograph it or one of the staff can and you will be assured of a quality photo at no charge. I've seen collectors spend hundreds of dollars for professional photos of coins that wound up being worth only face value.

Sending a rubbing is a third matter where you need some instruction. A pencil rubbing of a coin will not survive a trip through the mail. Neither will a foil rubbing. Both need special protection. A foil rubbing comes out of the envelope looking like it had been flattened with a steam iron. The pencil rubbings are blurred and just as useless.

Both need protection from contact with the envelope. The simplest way is to take the rubbings and put them in a reversed (folded the other way) 2x2 cardboard holder, stapled on the open sides just like a coin. To be even more certain, put the rubbing loose in a small flat plastic box, or something similar, such as a matchbox.

Another problem, one I'm sure is not limited to the coin hobby, is the collector who has made a discovery and is afraid to ask because it might set off a stampede before he or she has a chance to find other examples. I can tell you from personal experience that you could count the instances of that happening on the fingers of one hand and have several fingers left over. The person making the discovery usually is the only one who directly benefits from the discovery.

Along the same lines is the person who discovers a potentially valuable coin and instead of reporting it, waits for someone else to report it. Security aside, this is exactly the wrong direction to proceed. If you are the first to report a new variety or other important find, your name goes into the record books as the discoverer. Letting George do it takes all the fun and excitement out of discovery. Unfortunately, there are scores of collectors who fit this description to a T.

Others are afraid to ask, fearing attracting attention to their collecting interests. Despite the fact that I never use an address, writers repeatedly ask me not to use their address. I'm a professional and I treat your correspondence in a professional manner. I never use an address without the specific permission of the writer. Very often I will use only the first name, because anyone with five minutes of time can find a home address for a family name on the Internet.

For example, there are 16 Alan Herberts listed on one popular search engine, including two Sir Alan Herberts - one in England and one in Australia. As it happens, they have the wrong address for me, so an Internet listing is not a serious problem, but it can be for someone with an uncommon name.

Always direct your inquiry to a specific person or a specific column. More than half of my mail comes in without my name in the address, meaning it has to go through two or three hands before it gets to me.

Put your full - not an abbreviation - city address on your envelope and on the letter inside. You may know what "JVL" in your return address means, but I may not know that you mean Jacksonville. Print both your name and address on the envelope and especially the letter. Your signature is often unreadable. Invest in address labels if your handwriting is as bad as mine. Put one on the letter and one on the envelope. Some even include a third address label to be used on the return envelope, but that's not necessary.

Use the proper state abbreviations in your address and our address. More than half of the incoming letters have at least one mistake in the addresses, which helps to delay the mail. Most schools are still teaching the old uppercase - lowercase abbreviations with periods that went out with high-button shoes. The U.S. Postal Service two-letter state abbreviations - both upper case with no periods - are what you need to learn. If your school is still using the old ones, jump up and down until they change.

Read the instructions. Reread the instructions. If a self-addressed stamped envelope (SASE) is requested, make sure it is a full size, legal size #9 or #10 envelope. I hate small envelopes for several reasons. They tend to get lost in the mail. When writing for information, much of it is prepared on full size 8½ x 11-inch sheets that don't fit well in small envelopes - or surplus Christmas card envelopes - and cost a surcharge if the small envelope is too thick. As a general rule, a first class stamp will cover three sheets of paper and a long envelope. Remember, when you write to anyone, even a commercial firm, you are asking a favor and the best way to get it is to follow the rules.

To avoid all these problems, I personally ask that you send a loose, unused, first-class stamp with your question. Even those are a problem when you cut the backing so close to the stamp that it's impossible to separate. Return postage is a mark of courtesy when writing to anyone for information. You don't need to staple or tape the stamp, as it won't get out of the envelope. In a few cases, the instructions are ignored and an enclosed envelope has much more postage than is needed. Ignore the request for return postage at your peril! Your letter goes to the bottom of the stack.

If your letter to F+W is on more than one topic - paying a subscription or other business - put the question on a separate sheet of paper, addressed to me, in an envelope with the return postage. There will be delays if everything is on one piece of paper. There are more than 400 people working in Iola, Wisconsin, and letters do get separated from the envelope. Don't forget to date the letter, as I sort incoming mail by date.

Here's another rule - very, very important. Never send a coin or other valuable without writing first for instructions. I cannot, and F+W Publications cannot, accept responsibility for unsolicited material. You would be surprised at the number of people who violate this rule, many not even including return postage. Mail addressed to me at the Iola address has to be forwarded, adding to the hazard of improper packing.

To see what improper packing means, take an envelope and put a loose nickel inside it. Hold the envelope by the opposite corner and snap it. You'd better do this outside as the nickel is going to fly a considerable distance, slicing its way right through the paper.

The kicker that makes this rule doubly important is the second reason for not sending unsolicited material to anyone. Under postal regulations, any unsolicited merchandise may be treated as a gift. This means that you are under no obligation to pay for address labels, calendars - or coins that you didn't agree to in advance.

I don't appraise coins. I do want to see new minting varieties, but you need to write or e-mail first, as I have specific mailing instructions, return postage and an exam fee if we don't use the coin in one of the F+W publications.

By now you have learned some of the basics of being a collector. From here on I'm going to explain some of the terms you will run into as I go along. As you probably have noticed, I've used several terms that you are not likely to be familiar with. If I don't get to your particular term, there's a glossary in the back.

Chapter 14

MINTMARKS

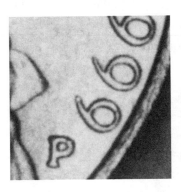

One of the first things you will run into when you start collecting coins is the mention or reference to a mintmark. A mintmark is a symbol or marking that designates the specific mint where the coin was struck. The U.S. uses letters. Other countries use letters, numbers or symbols to identify their mints.

At the present time, there are four U.S. mints using mintmarks on our coins. The main mint at Philadelphia uses a "P" on all but the cent, while Denver uses a "D," San Francisco uses an "S" and West Point uses a "W." At one time or another we had mints at Carson City, NV, using "CC," Dahlonega, GA, using "D" and Charlotte, NC, using a "C." Note that the Denver and Dahlonega mints operated during different time periods, so there was no conflict in using the D mintmark.

Mintmarks are found on either the obverse (front) or reverse (back) of the coin, but since the 1960s they have been standardized on the obverse of U.S. coins. Collectors paid little attention to mintmarks until about the 1900 era.

Mintmarks on various U.S. coins.

Q: *What part of a coin is the exergue?*

A: *It's that part of the design below the main design on the reverse of a coin that carries details such as the date and place of minting. It is sometimes separated from the main design by a raised line.*

Mintmarks are usually the second thing that collectors look at on a coin. Don't forget to continue your routine on each coin you examine. Mintmarks are important because they allow you to match a coin to a specific listing in a price guide, where you will find the mintage figure for your coin.

Mintmarks on various U.S. coins.

Chapter 15

COLONIAL COINS

With this chapter I'm beginning to list specific coins that you can collect. Again I'm not recommending any particular coin to collect, just showing you what's out there.

An important segment of our coinage is Colonial coins, struck by several of the colonies before they were united. They have their own listings, separate from our federal coinage. A vital point - almost every Colonial coin has been copied and recopied. The overwhelming odds are that almost any Colonial piece you come in contact with (except from a dealer) is a worthless or near-worthless copy. Thousands upon thousands of fake Continental dollars and New England shillings are among the common copies.

The key advice here is to find a catalog and then find a dealer who specializes in Colonials. A dealer or a collector will be your only source for Colonial coins, so it's important to find someone who is willing to share their knowledge. If you are on the

A New England shilling

Internet, you can find a list of dealers by specialty at the American Numismatic Association Web site at www.money.org.

When considering a Colonial coin, check the edge. If there is a raised ridge of coin metal, or evidence it has been removed, then the piece is undoubtedly a worthless cast copy.

If Colonials catch your fancy and you can afford them, by all means, go ahead. Starting with something as difficult to collect should give you pause while you learn more about collecting in general.

U.S. Colonials

Chapter 16

HALF CENTS

Beginning with this chapter I'm going to briefly describe each federal denomination and some of the highlights of that particular coin.

Early U.S. half cents

A 1796 "No Pole" half cent

The half cent is the smallest denomination struck by the U.S. Mint. They were important to commerce, as in the early days there were a multitude of foreign coins in circulation with differing values, so that making change was often a real headache. The half cents were struck from 1793 to 1857, so you won't find one in circulation. Those with dates from 1840 to 1849 list at $1,000 in Good-4, the lowest acceptable grade.

There are five series designs for the half cents. The Liberty Cap was only struck in 1793. The Liberty Cap facing right was produced from 1794 to 1797. Next was the Draped Bust (1800-1808), the Classic Head (1809-1836) and the Braided Hair, struck from 1840 to the end of the denomination in 1857. Prices in Good-4 grade are all over the map, as high as $27,000 for the 1796 "No Pole" variety.

Chapter 17

ONE CENT

Q: *Why are there so few top grade 1814 cents?*

A: *Almost the entire output—357,830—was used for the Mint payroll, so nearly all of the cents struck that year circulated. Can you imagine the uproar if the Mint attempted to pay its employees with newly minted cents today?*

Early U.S. Large cents

You call them "pennies." but they are not pennies. They are cents. Right on the coin it says "ONE CENT." Penny is a throwback to our English heritage, as the English have used pennies for close to a thousand years. In the United States, it's a slang term that's impossible to eradicate. Even the Mint has thrown in the towel and refers to them as "pennies" in its literature.

The cent is an important coin for collectors. Up until recently, it was the most common coin to be found in a collector's hands. Most of our older collectors started with a cent coin board when they were young, working up from that to other denominations.

The Large cent wasn't called that until after 1857, when the series ended and the smaller diameter and lighter Flying Eagle cents were issued. The Large cent is unique in that three different designs were used in 1793, the first year of issue. The Flowing Hair cent with Chain reverse was the first, followed by the Flowing Hair with Wreath reverse and the Liberty Cap. A slightly different Liberty Cap was struck in 1795 and 1796. The Draped Bust cent finished 1796 and on to 1807, followed by the Classic Head design from 1808 to 1814.

A Flying Eagle cent

No cents were struck in 1815, the only break in that denomination. The Coronet design lasted from 1816 to 1839, followed by the Braided Hair cent from 1840 to the last Large cent in 1857.

The Flying Eagle cent began in 1856 with an estimated mintage of 2,500. Some 17.4 million were struck in 1857 and 24.6 million in 1858. The short series included an 1858/7 overdate and large- or small-motto 1858 varieties. All of the Flying Eagle cents were struck on copper-nickel planchets.

An Indian Head cent

The Flying Eagles were replaced in 1859 by the Indian Head cent, also on copper-nickel planchets. In 1860, a shield was added at the top of the reverse. There were three varieties for 1864, the shield reverse on copper nickel, and the same design on bronze, plus a design adding an L to the ribbon, identifying James Longacre as the designer.

A 1909-S VDB Lincoln cent

The Indian Head was replaced in 1909 by the Lincoln cent and lots of controversy. Victor David Brenner put his initials on the lower reverse of the 1909 cents, only to have it removed in mid-year and not restored until 1918 on the base of the bust on the obverse.

Design changes and minting varieties abound. The cent had a wheat-head wreath until 1958 and the Lincoln Memorial reverse since 1959. The modern Lincoln cent has a couple of outstanding hub-doubled coins, the 1955 and 1972, plus the large- and small-date 1960 cents. More on that in the chapter on minting varieties.

The cent holds the record for alloy changes. There were the copper Large cents, the copper-nickel Flying Eagles, the copper-nickel and bronze Indian Head cents, the bronze, brass and zinc-plated steel and the current copper-plated zinc on the Lincoln cent, making a total of six different metals or alloys. A common mistake at all levels is to refer to "copper" cents when the correct term (except for the Large cents) is copper alloy.

Above: Lincoln cent with Lincoln Memorial reverse. Below: 1972 doubled-die cent.

1960 large date type.

1960-D small date type.

Chapter 18

TWO CENTS

Some of you younger collectors may not even know that we once had a two-cent coin, as well as a three-cent coin. The two-cent was introduced in 1864 as the Civil War was starting to wind down. It was struck until 1873, so it's also a very short series. Two varieties of note: The 1864 comes with Large or Small Motto and also comes with various amounts of rotation of the reverse die. Turn the coin over top to bottom to catch the rotations.

Two-cent coin

The Large Motto and Small Motto two cent

Chapter 19

THREE CENTS

The three-cent coins came in two flavors - copper-nickel and silver. The silver came first, in three distinct varieties between 1851 and 1873. The Type 1 had no outline of the star. It was replaced in 1854 by the Type 2 with three outlines and again in 1859 with the Type 3 with two outlines.

The first ones were only 75 percent silver, but fell into line as a 90 percent silver coin in 1854.

Silver three-cent piece

Copper-nickel three-cent coin

The copper-nickel three-cent coin production overlapped part of the silver, beginning in 1865 and ending in 1889. Both kinds were cordially disliked by the public because of their small size - both are smaller than a dime - which made them easy to lose. However, their popularity with collectors is readily apparent when you read their price chart.

Chapter 20

HALF DIMES AND FIVE-CENT NICKELS

Our five-cent coin has been called a nickel ever since 1866, when it was first introduced. The earliest form of a five-cent coin was the silver half dimes.

The half dimes were among the first coins struck by the U.S. Mint in 1793 and maintained an odd 89.2 percent silver content until mid-1837, when another 0.8 percent silver brought them up to full strength.

The half dime minting varieties would keep any collector hopping. There are a large group of large or small dates, large or small 5C and even an inverted date in the denomination, which ended in 1873. Like the larger-denomination silver coins, it went through the Flowing Hair, Draped Bust with small eagle, Draped Bust with Heraldic Eagle and Liberty Cap. Then came the Seated Liberty with no stars, with stars, drapery added to left elbow, arrows at date, arrows removed and the final issues from 1860 to 1873 with UNITED STATES OF AMERICA replacing the stars.

An early half dime

A copper-nickel five-cent Shield nickel

The five-cent nickel, actually copper-nickel, was a pleasant surprise for mint officials, as it was gladly accepted by the public, in marked contrast to the usual scorn greeting new designs. The chief grumble was the incorrect presumption that the 1866 design intentionally glorified the stars and bars of the Confederacy.

Following the Shield design of 1866-1882 were the Liberty nickels of 1883-1913. That series had the distinction of a major variety at beginning and end - the 1883 "No Cents" and the five clandestine 1913 nickels now worth more than a million dollars each.

An 1883 nickel without "CENTS"

One of five 1913 Liberty nickels

Then came the Indian Head nickel, quickly renamed Buffalo by the public for the big buffalo on the reverse, avoiding confusion with the Indian Head cents still very much in circulation. Two major varieties in this series are the 1918/1917-D overdate and the 1937-D three-legged buffalo. The design was changed in 1913, removing the mound the buffalo stands on.

The Jefferson nickel is still with us, starting in late 1938 after the last of the Buffalo nickels were struck. Included in this series are the war-time nickels with a low-grade silver alloy replacing precious copper and a very large mintmark over the dome on the reverse. Years later, a 1943/1942 overdate was discovered.

The 1913 Buffalo nickel

1939 Jefferson nickel

Popular with collectors are fully struck coins with complete steps on the reverse. Some dates with five or six full steps are rare to extremely rare.

Riding on the popularity of the State quarters, a group of four new designs have been released, honoring the Lewis and Clark expedition. The Buffalo reappeared on the reverse of the 2005 nickels, turned 180 degrees to face right rather than left.

Jefferson has a new look, as well.

The 2005 Lewis and Clark nickel with a new portrait of Jefferson and the buffalo reverse.

Q: *Which minor coin was the first with the E PLURIBUS motto?*

A: *That honor goes to the Liberty head, or "V" nickel, introduced in 1883. It's interesting to note that early coins carried the E PLURIBUS UNUM motto without any specific law requiring it. The requirement was made law in 1873, and the nickel was the first minor coin affected.*

Chapter 21

THE 10-CENT DIME

An early dime

They didn't get around to striking the first dimes until 1796, but a slow start has been followed by tremendous production figures. Not exactly a popular coin, it still figures prominently in commerce. It, too, didn't reach 90-percent silver until 1837, going through several designers. While a 10-cent coin was authorized, the coins never carried more than 10C to identify the denomination.

The first were called dismes, until 1837 when the official denomination on the coin became "dime." Like the half dimes, there are numerous varieties, with large- and small-date digits and 10C and overdates. The first ones carried the Small Eagle reverse and matched the half dimes from then on. There were two periods of arrows added to the date 1853-1855 and 1873-1874, the first for a slight decrease, the latter indicating a slight increase in weight. The series was replaced by the Barber dime in 1892, the Mercury dime in 1916 and the Roosevelt dime in 1946. The latter, like the designs for the quarter, changed from silver to copper-nickel clad on a copper core in 1965.

The Roosevelt dime has been with us since 1946, honoring President Franklin D. Roosevelt and his connection with the March of Dimes for polio. It made the transition from 90-percent silver to copper-nickel clad copper in 1965, although silver dimes dated 1964 were struck into 1966.

Franklin D. Roosevelt on the dime

A 1982 dime without a mintmark

Proof dimes have received more than their share of attention, with several dates appearing with a missing S mintmark. Some 1982 circulation dimes also got out without a mintmark, the only known circulation date and denomination where this has happened. This also happened to some proof nickels and the 1990 No-S proof cent.

Chapter 22

THE 20-CENT DOUBLE DIME

The short-lived U.S. 20-cent piece.

At first glance, a 20-cent coin seems to be an oddball denomination, but it actually fits our decimal coinage. It's the 25-cent coin that really is a misfit. The coin picked up its "double dime" nickname early on.

Regardless of status, the coin simply was not popular and ended up on the scrap heap after a very brief appearance from 1875-1878. The key coin of this series, both in numbers and values, is the 1878-CC that shows very strong hub doubling and has sold for as much as $148,500.

Chapter 23

THE QUARTER DOLLAR

The quarter dollar, or "quarter" as it is universally called, started as a 25-cent coin. Actually, the first quarters struck in 1796 didn't show a denomination. 25C was added in 1804 and lasted until 1838, replaced by "QUAR.DOL." The full wording wasn't spelled out until the Barber quarters of 1892. Like the dime, production began with the Small Eagle reverse. The sequence of series was different following the Draped Bust, Heraldic Eagle. The Liberty Cap (1815-1828) design had E PLURIBUS UNUM above the eagle. It was removed in 1831 and the Seated Liberty design began in 1838. The "no drapery" design lasted three years (1838-1840), followed by the "added drapery" variety used from 1840 on.

Early bust quarter designs. Above: Small Eagle. Below: Large Eagle.

A 1918/1917-S overdate

The "Arrows at date" obverse lasted only three years - 1853-1855. The rays on the reverse - added at the same time - were removed in 1854. In 1866, the motto IN GOD WE TRUST appeared on a ribbon above the eagle. It remained, while the Arrows were added to the date in 1873-1874 and removed again in 1875. Again, there was a slight reduction for the earlier Arrows and a slight increase in weight when they were removed. The Barber quarters came along in 1892, succeeded by the Standing Liberty quarter (with TRVST like the later Peace dollar) in 1916.

The first Standing Liberty design had Liberty's right breast exposed - not a wardrobe malfunction - but an intentionally classic design. The robe was closed in 1917 and the eagle was moved up to make room for three stars.

The quarter is replete with die varieties, making it a mecca for collectors. Perhaps most famous is the 1918/1917-S overdate, one of several for the denomination, catalogued with a full head for $300,000.

The Washington quarter has been with us since 1932. It was intended to be a one-year circulating commemorative. However, unexpected public demand again affected production and the Mint resumed striking them in 1934. In recent years it has become the preferred coin of commerce. This leads us to today and the next chapter on the State quarters.

A commemorative 1932 Washington quarter

Q: *Was the Washington quarter really a commemorative coin?*

A: *Yes. It was originally intended to be a one-year issue in 1932, but was popular enough to be continued. That popularity with the public is in marked contrast to many other new issues. Production was resumed in 1934, so there were none struck in 1933.*

Chapter 24

THE REMARKABLE STATE QUARTERS

The Royal Canadian Mint can take credit for an idea that has turned on millions of new collectors in the United States. The U.S. Mint watched the popular success of the 1992 Canadian quarters honoring the 12 parts of the country from Alberta to Yukon. They decided on an ambitious 50-coin program spread over 10 years to recognize each state in the Union.

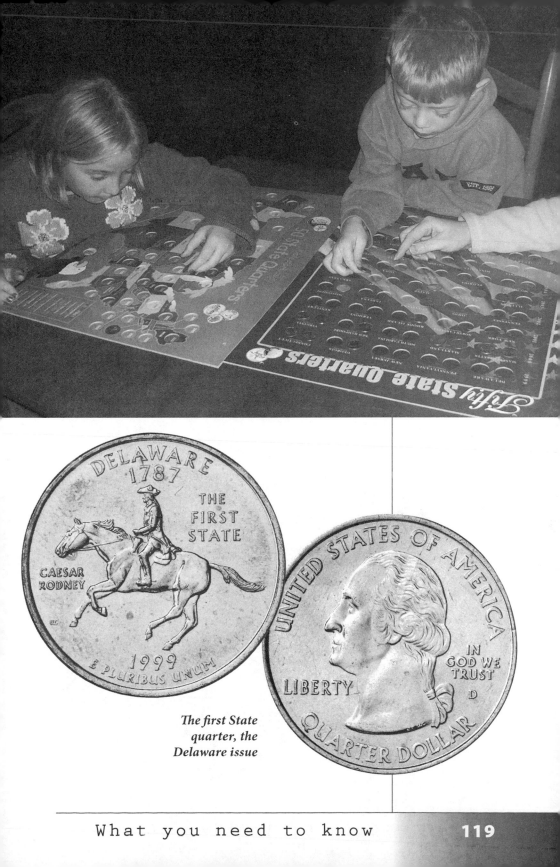

The first State
quarter, the
Delaware issue

Connecticut

Pennsylvania

New Jersey

Georgia

Massachusetts

Maryland

South Carolina

New Hampshire

Virginia

New York

North Carolina

Rhode Island

Vermont

Kentucky

Tennessee

Ohio

Louisiana

Indiana

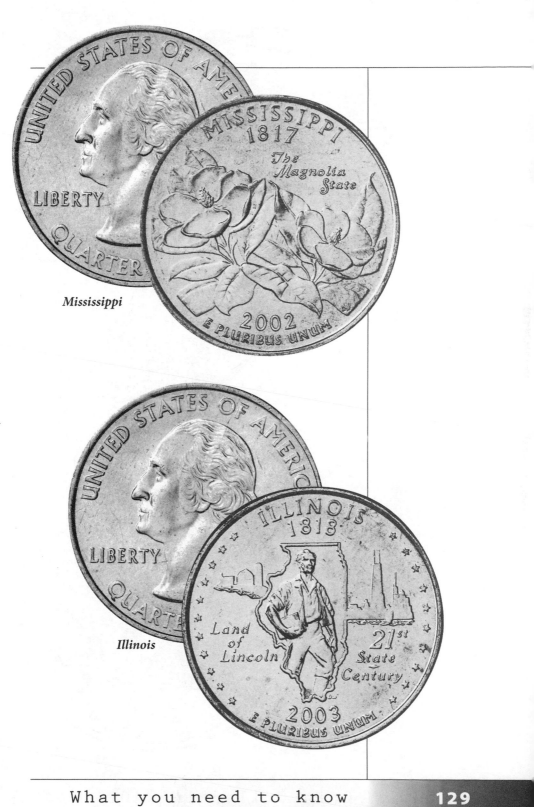

Mississippi

Illinois

Alabama

Maine

Missouri

Arkansas

Michigan

Florida

Texas

Iowa

Wisconsin

California

Minnesota

Oregon

*1976
Bicentennial
quarter*

The first five coins were issued in 1999, honoring the first five states to enter the Union. Five more will be issued each year, about every two months, through 2008.

Committees from each state selected the designs to be submitted to the Mint for a final selection. Several states have allowed public voting on the designs.

Sales of the coins have been substantial. The Mint estimates that some 145 million people are collecting the State quarters. Not just from their own state, but from every state that has a new coin. Anecdotal evidence supports the Mint figure.

I can speak from personal experience, as there are ample signs that there is a remarkable upsurge in the collecting community. I gave a talk on coins to a Masonic group. There were about 20 men, all in their 50s or older. I asked for a show of hands if they were collecting State quarters for themselves, their children or their grandchildren. Every hand in the room went up.

One word of caution. Some collectors carry a series like this too far, removing from circulation every State quarter they find. There are numerous collectors who have thousands of dollars tied up in the coins. You need only to look at the record amounts of bags and rolls being sold by the Mint.

The hard facts are that with so many collectors doing this, there will be a surplus of these coins for decades to come. You need only look at the Bicentennial coins, which went through the same collecting frenzy in 1976. The quarter still hasn't reached a $1 value for a 30-year old MS-60 grade specimen.

My standard advice is to collect only those coins you need to complete the series and to fill the family albums. Collect them in the best grade possible, preferably the highest possible uncirculated grade. It should tell you something that almost 40 years later, we don't list any values for circulated Bicentennial quarters. Cash in 15 or 20 of the circulated coins and buy a MS-65 grade for your collection.

As with any special coin prices for State quarter minting varieties have gone through the roof. As one example, all five of the 1999 State quarters from both the Philadelphia and Denver Mints were found with rotated reverses, some as much as 180 degrees, or half a circle. Prices for the larger rotations peaked for a short time in the $500 range. As this is being written, we have three die varieties of the Wisconsin quarter. Sets of the three are selling for as much as $1,100. Off-center strikes, double strikes and other significant minting varieties are bringing large multiples of the same thing on an ordinary Washington quarter. See the chapter on Minting Varieties.

Chapter 25

Half Dollars

Early bust half dollar designs. Above: Flowing Hair. Below: Draped Bust.

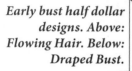

Like the other denominations, the early half dollars, first struck in 1794, had a broad spectrum of die varieties. Large or small letters or digits, overdates and several different designs over the years give the half, which used to be a mainstay of commerce, a rich past. Like the half dime, the half dollar started with the Flowing Hair design (1794-1795), followed by the Draped Bust, Small Eagle (1796-1797) and the Draped Bust, Heraldic Eagle (1801-1807). In 1807, the Bust half with 50C was introduced, lasting until 1836, with a very lengthy list of overdates and other minting varieties. The design continued, but with 50 CENTS spelled out (1836-1837).

More classic bust design half dollars. Top: "50 C" Middle: "50 Cents" Bottom: "Half Dollar"

For 1838-1839, the change was to HALF DOL. The Seated Liberty series ran from 1839 to 1853 when Arrows were added to the date along with Rays around the eagle reverse. Like the quarter, the Rays were removed in 1854 and the Arrows disappeared in 1856. In 1866, the ribbon with IN GOD WE TRUST was added above the eagle. The Arrows came back for 1873-1874 and left again in 1875, again weight related.

Seated Liberty half dollar

Q: *Over the years I have seen several reports of the finding of 1915 dated Standing Liberty halves, but never an explanation of where they come from. What happened?*

A: *As is the case with most "unknown" dates of United States coins, the 1915 pieces turned up, but got turned down when experts examined them and determined that they were 1935 dated pieces that had the 3 cleverly altered into a 1. Apparently all of the reported specimens came from a single source. Trust the mint reports in most catalogs; if they don't list a date or mint, it means there were no coins officially struck for that date or mint.*

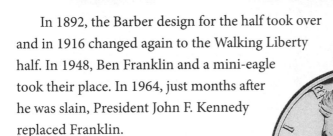

Barber half dollar

In 1892, the Barber design for the half took over and in 1916 changed again to the Walking Liberty half. In 1948, Ben Franklin and a mini-eagle took their place. In 1964, just months after he was slain, President John F. Kennedy replaced Franklin.

Like the other larger-denomination coins, the halves started with less than 90- percent silver before the long-term issue at that level. When silver prices got out of control in the early 1960s, the rest of the coins turned to copper-nickel clad on copper cores, but the half dollar retained a 40 percent share of silver from 1965 through 1970 before joining the rest of the coins. Since 1965, all of the denominations have at one time or another been minted in 40 percent or 90 percent silver. One type of proof set now carries 90-percent silver coins again.

Due to a lack of demand from the public the half dollar is slowly dying. Mintage figures are down sharply as the quarter takes its place as the favorite commercial coin.

Kennedy half dollar

Chapter 26

Dollars

The silver dollars matched the first Flowing Hair design (1794-1795), the Draped Bust, Small eagle (1796-1798), Draped Bust Heraldic eagle (1798-1804), Seated Liberty, No Motto (1840-1866), and the Seated Liberty with IN GOD WE TRUST above the eagle (1866-1873).

The old silver dollars were just about the most unloved coins in our pockets, except in small areas in the West and South. The new, small-size Anthony and Sacagawea dollars are just about the most unloved coins in our pockets today.

Get the picture? The public does not like and even hates a dollar coin.

Draped bust dollar

Seated Liberty dollar

Morgan silver dollar

Q: *I recently purchased some trade dollars from a private source in Asia. What effect will the chop marks have on the value?*

A: *They will reduce the value, but a more serious problem is the probability that you may have bought counterfeit coins, as Asia is a major source of fakes, especially copies of U.S. coins, made for the tourist trade. There are reputable Asian coin dealers of course, but a man came to me recently with five silver dollars, purchased in Singapore, three Morgans and two Trade dollars. All were fakes and didn't even contain any silver. They had been subjected to fire and other applications to give them an "aged" appearance. He told me that the dealer had "hundreds" more in his shop. I would urge that you submit all of your coins to be authenticated. Beware of the bargain or "fire sale" prices.*

Trade dollar

Unfortunately, the U.S. Mint has several times ignored history. They produced the Trade dollar (1873-1885), which turned into a major scandal. In 1878, the Morgan dollar came on the scene, lasting with gaps until 1921, when the Peace dollar began. That lasted officially until 1935, but 1964-D dollars were struck with the Peace design and then destroyed.

Q: *Why were there so many ads back in the 1970s offering "silver" Ike circulation strike dollars?*

A: *The two principal causes were ignorance or an attempt to play on public gullibility. The ads pretty much stopped when the silver price reached the point where the public was aware of the difference. However, with an entire new generation growing up in the meantime, there are plenty of people today who think the Ikes were 90 percent silver like the Morgans and Peace dollars. The proof and special uncirculated Ikes, those with an S mintmark, are 40 percent silver, but the rest are copper-nickel clad on a copper core.*

The Peace dollar

The Eisenhower "Ike" dollar

The Susan B. Anthony dollar

Sacagawea "golden" dollar

They reincarnated the Ike dollar in silver-dollar size in (1971-1978) - a flop - and the near quarter-size Anthony (1979-1981, 1999) that logically got spent as quarters. Most went directly from the customers right back to the banks. The Sacagawea dollars were struck beginning in 2000. The only happy people are the collectors who have made the silver Peace and Morgan dollars one of the most popular collectibles.

Production of silver dollars as bullion resumed in 1986 and for commemorative coins, resumed in 1982.

Chapter 27

GOLD COINS

Gold coins were the mainstay of our economy from the very beginning of our nation. Although all but the smallest denominations were beyond the reach of the average person, banks used them as assets. Gold was discovered in a number of places and much of it was converted to coinage.

Most of the public didn't need gold coins in a period when a $5 or $10 gold coin was a month's wages. The banks got the most benefit - assets that were compact and easily stored.

The $1 gold was first struck in 1849 with the Type I Liberty Head. The Indian Head or Type II lasted from 1854-1856, replaced by the Type III Indian Head, last struck in 1889. They were unpopular because of their small size.

Gold Liberty Head dollar

*Liberty Cap 2 1/2
Dollar gold piece*

Turban Head 2 1/2 Dollar gold piece

Classic Head 2 1/2 Dollar gold piece

Coronet Head 2 1/2 Dollar gold piece

Indian Head 2 1/2 Dollar gold piece

U.S. 3 dollar gold piece

The $2.50 or Quarter Eagle was struck beginning in 1796 as the Liberty Cap. In 1808, the Turban Head appeared, modified in 1809 with stars above the smaller head. In 1829, the diameter was reduced. The Classic head appeared in 1834 with a reduction in fineness. The Coronet Head (1840-1907) settled on .900 fine. The Indian Head was struck from 1908 to 1929.

The $3 gold was intended to pay for a sheet of 100 three-cent stamps. Other uses were found and the coin was struck from 1854 to 1889.

Liberty Cap 5 dollar gold piece – "small eagle" type

Q: *What happened to gold coin collections in 1933?*

A: When President Roosevelt ordered all gold coins returned to the government there was an exemption of up to $100 face value that could be retained in a collection. However, many ignored the law despite threatened fines and jail sentences. The recall had little or no effect on the tons of gold coins in European banks.

Liberty Cap 5 dollar gold piece – "large eagle" type

Turban Head 5 dollar gold piece

Classic Head 5 dollar gold piece

Coronet Head 5 dollar gold piece

Coronet Head 5 dollar gold piece – "In God We Trust" added

Indian Head 5 dollar gold piece

The $5 Half Eagle began with the Liberty Cap, and Small or Heraldic Eagle in 1795. The Turban Head Capped Draped Bust replaced it in 1807 and in turn was followed by the Turban Head Capped Head in 1813, the Classic Head in 1834 and the Coronet Head in 1839. IN GOD WE TRUST was added on a ribbon above the eagle in 1866. The Indian Head took over in 1908 and was struck until 1929. Production of gold Eagles and fractional Eagles resumed as bullion coins in 1986 and commemoratives in 1984.

Liberty Cap 10 dollar gold piece
– "small eagle" type

Liberty Cap 10 Dollar gold piece – "large eagle" type

Q: *Is it true that a large quantity of the Type I gold dollars were melted down by the government?*

A: *There is some question as to the legality of the melt, as Congress did not authorize it, but Mint Director James Snowden did melt down 8,000,000 of the coins in 1860, and used the gold to strike the Type III and other gold coins.*

Coronet Head 10 Dollar gold piece

The $10 Eagle started with the Small eagle in 1795-1797 and, in sequence, the Heraldic eagle (1797-1804), Old Style Coronet Head (1838-1839), New Style Coronet Head (1839-1866) and continuing with the added IN GOD WE TRUST to 1907. The motto was removed from 1907-1908 and restored in 1909 with production until 1933.

In 1933, President Roosevelt used an Executive Order to call in gold, but only a fraction of the outstanding gold was recovered. Since then, gold has again become legal to own and the U.S. Mint regularly issues gold bullion coins.

Indian Head 10 dollar gold piece

Liberty Head Double Eagle – No motto, "Twenty D." below eagle.

Liberty Head Double Eagle – Motto added, "Twenty Dollars" below eagle.

Saint-Gaudens Double Eagle
– no motto below eagle.

Like the $1 gold, the $20 gold Double Eagle didn't start until 1849, with one known for that year. In part of 1861, a different Paquet reverse was used, creating another rarity. The Longacre reverse was resumed in 1862. IN GOD WE TRUST was added in 1866. In 1877, the TWENTY D. was changed to TWENTY DOLLARS.

In 1907-1908, the motto was removed, returning in 1909. The Saint-Gaudens design was used from 1907 to 1933. The one official survivor of the 1933 mintage sold in 2002 for $7,590,000.

The Paquet reverse on a gold Double Eagle

Saint-Gaudens
$20 gold

Today, gold coins are expensive collectibles, even though many can be bought for little more than the melt value of the coins. It's the melt value that keeps the cost up.

Gold is a popular investment. However, don't jump in before you read the chapter on investments. Close your checkbook and sit on it, firmly.

Q: *How do I go about converting carats of gold to fineness?*

A: *Pure gold is 24 carat, so the scale figures out like this: A single carat is .0416 fine, 12 carat gold is .500 fine, 18 carat gold is .750 fine. Most gold jewelry is figured in carats so using these figures it is a simple matter to determine the full weight of the piece, dividing by the fineness to figure the amount of gold that it contains. Many coins are 22 karat gold, thus with a fineness of .9166. The Gold Stamping Act of 1976 specifies that all jewelry made and sold after Oct. 1, 1981, must be within 0.3 percent of the specific stamped content, or about 1/14th of a carat, according to the Gold Institute. While this is not a guarantee that what you buy is correctly labeled, it does give you recourse if you find that the product was mislabeled. One of the popular methods of describing fineness up until about the late 1940s was the use of fractions of a carat, which was divided into 32 parts. Thus a coin's fineness might be described as 21 and 19/32 carat gold, which corresponds with the now common and easy to use .900 fine.*

Chapter 28

COMMEMORATIVE COINS

Most commemoratives are intended for collectors. The appearance of circulating commemoratives, such as the Washington quarter, the Eisenhower dollar and the State quarters has changed the commemorative market, because now it is possible to find a commemorative in your pocket change. This used to be the way almost all coins were collected. The U.S. Mint and other world mints have discovered that making commemoratives is a good way to plump up the bottom line. They have also learned that overselling the market leads to sharply declining profits. Several private mints closed their doors after failing to learn this lesson.

From the collector's viewpoint, commemoratives are noted for the wide range of topics. Whether you collect coins with oil wells or race cars or ships or planes, you can find the commemoratives that suit your desires. Repeating a word of warning, beware of so-called commemorative "coins" that are actually medals struck by private mints. The definition of a coin is simple - a piece issued by a government body and assigned a specific value for commerce. If the piece in question doesn't match the definition, then it's not a coin.

An 1892 Columbian Exhibition commemorative

When you are reading a price guide, you will probably find the commemoratives in separate sections. U.S. commemoratives come in two groups - those from 1892 to 1954 and those made since 1982. The former group is responsible for the gap between 1954 and 1982, when Congress tired of the abuses of the commemorative programs and refused to authorize any more. They relented enough to produce the circulating Bicentennial coins of 1976, and six years later the 1982 Washington half dollar commemorative restarted the program with much different rules. There are several excellent books on commemorative coins that you will want for your library.

A $10 gold 1992 Olympic commemorative

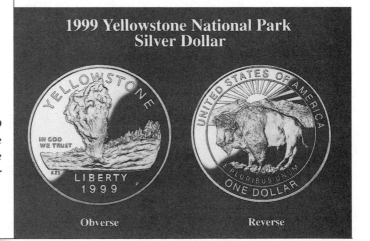

The 1999 Yellowstone commemorative dollar

Chapter 29

PROOF AND MINT SETS

A U.S. proof set

The original purpose of a proof coin was to test the dies to make sure the design was complete and would strike up properly. Modern proofs are sold as collectibles, even though they are legal tender. There are two main types of proofs - the mirror, or brilliant surface coins that we Americans like, and matte proofs, generally favored by European collectors.

A U.S. Prestige set

A matte proof coin

Brilliant or mirror proofs are strictly defined as being struck two or more times with polished dies on polished planchets. The central design is often frosted, making a sharp contrast to the mirror fields. Such proofs have their own grading system, as well as adjectival criteria such as "Deep Mirror" or "Cameo" proofs.

Matte proofs have the same sharp edges on the design elements, but the surface is rough, in some cases even produced by sand blasting. The relatively few U.S. matte proofs are difficult to separate from the similar circulation strikes, except for the sharp-edged design elements.

Common misconceptions about proofs include the tendency to call proof a grade, when it is actually a condition of manufacture. Don't feel bad if you have been misusing, it as a majority of collectors also mistakenly use condition when they mean grade for circulating coins.

Another frequent mistake is to mislabel a proof coin that has circulation wear or damage as a "circulated" coin. The rule is: "Once a proof, always a proof." Any proof showing wear is classed as an impaired proof. Quite a few proof coins show up in circulation for a number of reasons. The most common include coins discarded by dealers who open sets and select the better-grade coins to sell individually. Many a collection has been either stolen outright or rifled by children looking for candy money. For more detail, read the ANA Grading Guide at the end of the book.

One of the fads of the 1960s is showing up again. The hook is "unopened mint packaging" with a small premium over opened packaging. There are two problems with this. One, you have no idea whether there really is a proof or mint set in that box, which could have been steamed open to remove the set and replace it with washers.

Two, you may be missing out on a valuable minting variety, such as the missing mintmarks on several proof coins. I repeat an old Yankee proverb at every opportunity - "Don't buy a pig in a poke." A poke is defined as a sack. Sight unseen in this case is bad business.

Don't be surprised if you find more circulation strikes than proofs for a given date - and prices to match. Collectors, if given a choice, tend to want proofs, leaving larger quantities in their hands with consequently lower prices.

You can easily fill a shelf in your library with books about proof coins. Be sure to have at least one book that fully explains the minting process by which all coins are made.

Q: *What is the difference between a mint set and a mint-packaged set?*

A: *A mint set is defined as a group of coins for one year from one mint, usually including all the coins struck in that year at that mint. A mint-packaged set is the same, except that the government mint specifically packaged it. The key difference is that anyone can assemble (and sell) a mint set.*

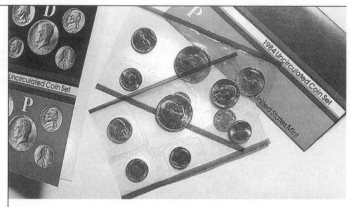

A mint-packaged mint set.

Mint sets consist of examples of all the coins struck at all of the mints in a given year. Privately assembled mint sets may contain the same coins as a mint-packaged set, but usually the mint-packaged sets will sell at a premium. The coins in a mint-packaged set have had at least some special care, but are usually difficult to distinguish from ordinary circulation strikes.

The Mint skipped making any mint-packaged mint sets in 1982 and 1983 as an economy measure. They resumed the sets in 1984 due to heavy pressure from collectors. Many privately packaged sets were made for those two years or a combination of souvenir sets from the two mints were sold by dealers to fill the gap.

The souvenir sets contain all the coins from a given mint for a given year and were sold only over the counter at the mints. They are not recognized or listed in coin price guides because the Mint failed to keep any records of the numbers sold. When buying a mint set, make sure it is a mint-packaged set and not a substitute, and it should be priced accordingly.

A privately packaged mint set.

Q: *I was told to buy proofs, as "then you won't have to worry about grading." Now I'm beginning to wonder.*

A: *With good reason. Proof is not a grade to begin with, but proofs are graded, and the ANA grading standards cover grades from impaired proofs up through proof-60 to proof-70, so you need to learn to grade proofs just like other coins.*

Q: *I have a couple of proof coins that are worn, as if they had been in circulation. How do you classify them?*

A: *"Once a proof, always a proof," to paraphrase an old saw. A proof coin remains a proof, as proof is not a grade, regardless of what happens to it. A circulated or damaged proof is classed as an "impaired" proof. This hasn't always been the case, as an old auction catalog lists a coin as follows: "Was a proof, now uncirculated."*

Q: *What is meant by a business strike coin?*

A: *Coins intended to circulate in commerce are described as either circulation strikes or business strikes. The two terms have the same meaning, with business strikes probably tracing to the banker's use of the term for their business customers.*

Q: *When were the first U.S. proof sets offered for sale?*

A: *Breen quotes an 1858 notice by J. R. Snowden, offering sets for sale, but George F. Jones, in the Coin Collectors Manual of 1860, says that cased sets were sold as early as the 1840s. A set of minor coins with a face value of $1.94 sold for $2.02.*

Chapter 30

MINTING VARIETIES

A very popular area of coin collecting is collecting minting varieties. They are usually given a blanket title of "errors," but there are actually three primary areas of minting varieties - intentional, wear and tear, and errors. There are more than 400 separate, defined classes of minting varieties. They are divided into the three principal areas - planchet, die and strike, in the PDS System that I originated in 1972. The PDS System is almost universally used throughout the minting-variety area of the hobby.

A 1955 doubled-die Lincoln cent

A 1972 doubled-die Lincoln cent

A coin struck on a planchet with a large clip.

A Jefferson nickel with a double-clipped planchet.

In brief, intentional classes include deliberate overdates or other design changes. Wear and tear on equipment and dies produce die cracks, die breaks and other changes, such as weak or missing design elements. Errors include various misstrikes, such as double-struck coins, brockages, wrong metal and other mistakes in the minting process.

The learning curve for minting variety collectors is quite steep and often hampered by the numerous slang terms and nicknames that are in common usage. If you do have an all-consuming thirst for the unexpected, this is certainly an area to explore. I've covered it in the latest edition of my book, *The Official Price Guide to Mint Errors*, published by Random House.

For some time there has been a gradual, but steady, increase in the number of collectors interested in minting varieties. At one time, you could count the number of coin dealers who had experience with them on one hand. Today there has been a significant increase in the number of dealers and collectors in this segment. Where once you might have found one dealer at a large coin show, today you may find 15 or 20 or more.

Q: *I have a coin that has parts of the designs of a dime and parts of a cent. Can this happen in the mint?*

A: *From your description it's possible that you have a dime, which was struck a second time by the cent dies, giving it a possible value of several hundred dollars. I would suggest having it authenticated by a specialist. For a genuine dual denomination coin, this has to be the sequence, as a cent will not fit into the feed mechanism or the dime dies.*

The key difference between minting varieties and regular coins is that most minting varieties have instant value. You can find one and literally walk across the street and sell it to a coin dealer. Regular coins may take scores of years, even centuries, before they appreciate to a significant value.

A coin press

Collecting minting varieties requires a thorough knowledge of the minting process and what it can and can't do to a coin. It requires the ability to recognize mint-process results from accidental or deliberate damage. (Yes, people do deliberately mutilate coins, either for spite, or to sell to some novice as a "real error.") Even mint employees have been known to deliberately create "errors" for sport, waiting to see how many collectors fall for them.

One of the key rules for collecting minting varieties is to avoid anything that has been "helped," whether inside or outside the mint. An altered coin is usually not collectible. However, it's good to know that some alterations, such as the "hobo" nickels, are highly collectible. Ironically, those altered coins have been heavily copied in recent years.

Unfortunately, our space to discuss this favorite area of mine is very limited. Minting varieties can be very complex, so you'll need all the help you can get. I'll be glad to answer your questions if you will contact me through the address in the Resources chapter and follow the instructions.

Q: *Is there an official count of the 1972 hub-doubled cents?*

A: *Like almost every minting variety there is no official count because the coins were not spotted before they left the mint. At least nine dies, including one with master die doubling, are known for the date from Philadelphia, plus several from Denver. The die designated as #1 had an estimated die life of 50,000 to 100,000 strikes. Those figures are likely to be rather conservative, as normal die life at the time was about a million strikes per die pair. At one time we listed 18 dies for Philadelphia, but after further study, John Wexler and I determined that several of the listings were stages of the same dies, so the number was narrowed down to nine. The one with master die doubling has doubling, which appears on half of all the 1972 cents from all three mints.*

Q: *What's the difference between a type and a variety?*

A: *A type coin is a coin that is representative of a particular series or denomination, usually one that is obsolete. The term is also used for current coins to a lesser extent. For example, type coins for the Lincoln cent would be one of any date or mint with the wheat reverse and a second coin of any date or mint with the memorial reverse. A variety signifies a change of design, either intentional or accidental.*

Chapter 31

WORLD COINS

The vast majority of American collectors collect U.S. coins, with perhaps a side trip to Canadian, United Kingdom or Mexican coins. They want to stay on familiar ground, with legends and mottos preferably in English. While there is plenty to do collecting U.S. coins, there is a vast area of world coins that can be explored at your own pace.

A spectacular coin

Many collectors shy away from world coins because of language problems and probably fear of the unknown. If you spend the time to research it, it will no longer be unknown and you can more easily face problems that may crop up. Most collectors assume that minting methods in other countries are different and they don't trust mintage figures to be accurate. If you don't think the unknown is a factor, watch a planeload of Americans getting off in a foreign country. The majority will head right for the nearest McDonald's or Wendy's.

*1936 Canadian
Voyager dollar*

Mexican silver Onza

These are problems that are slowly fading away as more knowledge of the minting process is available. The majority of mints around the world use the same methods - and often the same equipment - to produce their coins. With the exception of a handful of countries, most are willing to post accurate mintage figures in published price guides. The best available price guide for world coins is the *Standard Catalog of World Coins*, published by F+W.

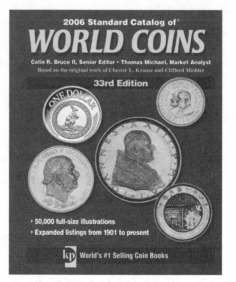

Standard Catalog of World Coins

This is the catalog that revolutionized collecting around the world, especially in Europe, as it was the first catalog to list coins of every country, in one language, with a multitude of photos of the coins. There had been other catalogs of world coins in the United States, but none that approached the scope and content of the *Standard Catalog*. The amazing thing is that it is continually being upgraded and enlarged as more information becomes available. Today the catalog is broken down by century, each coming in a thick telephone-book size that contains a wealth of information.

It may surprise you that some countries will not issue mintage figures or other information about their coins. The F+W Catalog Department depends on a network of collectors and dealers to contribute and provide missing information.

World Coin News

F+W also publishes the monthly *World Coin News*, which carries the latest news about new issues and information about other aspects of collecting world coins. For paper money collectors, there is the *Standard Catalog of World Paper Money* book and *Bank Note Reporter* monthly.

Chapter 32

BULLION COINS

An Austrian gold bullion coin

While there have been gold and silver coins around since the earliest coins appeared, the practice of selling bullion coins is a fairly recent development. The U.S., Canada, Austria and several other countries have used their production facilities to produce coins that are primarily an outlet for their stocks of precious metals.

An "art" bar

Q: *Why did the Treasury Department allow silver prices to increase? Wasn't the Treasury controlling prices?*

A: *The basic reason was that the Treasury didn't have enough silver to be able to hold the line on price. They removed price controls on silver in May 1967 and then ended redemption of Silver Certificates on June 24, 1968. While the Treasury was not responsible for the steep rise in 1980, the removal of the price controls actually laid the groundwork for the price increase.*

This actually started in the 1970s, when the big fad was "art bars" and "rounds." These were rectangles or round pieces made by any of the hundreds of private mints that sprang up. The art bars had a design of some kind on one or both flat surfaces, as did the rounds. The most popular were those that contained an ounce of silver, or that had some obvious mistake of fact.

The fad went away suddenly when the price of silver shot up to $52 an ounce in 1980. Hundreds of thousands of the silver pieces were sold to be melted. The private mints disappeared right along with their products. Today, there are only a very small handful of private mints still active.

A set of gold Eagles

With silver prices back down, the U.S. Mint got into the business, beginning in 1986 with their American Eagle Bullion Coins. Both silver dollars, containing an ounce of silver and gold Eagles in one-tenth, one-quarter, one-half and one-ounce sizes, denominated as $5, $10, $25 and $50, respectively, were issued. In 1997, the Mint added matching sizes of platinum coins. The key difference between these and those issued by the private mints is that the government coins are all legal tender for their face value. Not that anybody would be stupid enough to use them to buy a loaf of bread.

You no doubt are wondering what this has to do with coin collecting. Remember the bucket of sand? A small number of collectors have been buying these bullion coins in bulk quantities and treating them like any other coin, looking for those elusive few that will grade above MS-65. A very small number of them have been picked out this way that grade up into the rarified MS-66 to MS-69 area, and even an occasional MS-70 that goes for big bucks.

This, like other areas of collecting, comes close to being just another fad, so there is no guarantee that they will recoup their expense and time and show a profit.

Chapter 33

GRADING YOUR COINS

Grading is the watchword of today's hobby. Several third-party grading services have turned the art of grading into a major business.

Grading a coin means looking at the piece to determine the exact amount of wear. The old adjectival grading system is being replaced by a more accurate, better defined numerical grading system that uses a 70-point scale. The higher the number on this scale, the better the coin. As a result, in the upper grades, especially the Mint State

Q: *I have a coin that has a bad scar that I'd like to get repaired. Most of the dealers I've talked to say to leave the coin, which grades XF-40, alone, but I'd like to get it repaired. Any comments?*

I *think you've answered your own question with your dealer survey. Any repair work is only going to make matters worse, and anyone examining the repaired coin is going to suspect more than the visible alteration. It's best to leave it alone. It's your coin, so you can do as you wish with it, but a repaired coin is an altered coin.*

Q: *Why are there so many references in ads to "solder" on coins?*

A: *This is because in the early days coins were frequently used as jewelry, or buttons, and soldered to pins or other attachments. Solder is difficult to remove, and efforts to take it off frequently result in damage to the coin, which reduces the collector value. Reputable dealers will include the solder in the description of the coin.*

Q: *Has the Mint ever done a study on the amount of metal lost to wear on coins in circulation?*

A: *Several studies have been conducted over the years. One of the larger studies was conducted in 1886. From the measurements it was determined that a silver half dollar on average would lose 11 percent of its weight in 100 years, while the quarter would lose about 15 percent of its weight in the same period, reflecting the heavier use accorded the quarter even back then. Breaking these figures down, the average loss is one-ninth of a percent per year for the halves, and one-seventh of a percent per year for the quarters.*

(MS-60 to MS-70), a difference of a single point can mean a difference of hundreds or even thousands of dollars in collector value. This fact of life in the coin-collecting hobby underscores the importance of learning to grade coins yourself.

Unfortunately, there is no single standard for grading. Besides the original scale, instituted by the American Numismatic Association, each of the major grading firms has their own interpretation of the definitions for each grade. Most are nearly the same, but expressed in slightly different language. The often-subtle differences may extend to slightly different standards for different series of coins.

The best advice I can give here is to learn to grade coins yourself so you do not have to depend on a dealer or grading service to tell you what the

Q: *Does seawater affect silver coins?*

A: *Silver coins in salt water will start to corrode almost immediately. Many hoards from sunken ships are offered with "salt water" damage. An extended period of immersion will even damage the surface of a gold coin. However, the coins from the SS Central America suffered at worst only minor amounts of damage because of large quantities of iron nearby.*

grade is. When you reach the point where you can consistently grade within a single point, then you are far better equipped to buy coins for your collection. Since most coins are priced by their grade, you can save a substantial amount by being able to determine the actual grade of the coin. By learning to grade, you gain the knowledge to spot over-graded coins and also the rare bargains that have been under-graded.

As this is being written, the ANA is preparing the latest edition of the *Official ANA Grading Standards for U.S. Coins*, which should be available from book dealers or direct from the ANA. There are also several other grading books on the market.

Looking back at adjectival grading, the many terms used to describe coins often conflicted, and even more, often confused the potential buyer. A few took advantage of the system and used the multitude of terms to deliberately mislead the buyer. In many instances, it is necessary to query the dealer for a definition of a term before buying to ensure you are getting the grade you want.

Numerical grading is intended to cure these language problems for everyone's benefit. Many of us didn't like numerical grading when it was introduced in the early 1980s, but after seeing it in use, I am now satisfied that it is serving its purpose. Wait until you are comfortable with your grading ability before buying coins that you haven't had a chance to examine.

This is probably a good place for some specific advice. This rule states: "Don't be paranoid about your coins and their value." Almost every day I hear from collectors who refuse to put their coins in the mail, even though this is the principal method of getting coins to a grading service. (The only alternative is to go to a coin show where the service has a table.) One of the most frequent questions is: "Is there a grading service near where I live? The grading services do not accept walk-ins for their protection. Every day in this country, millions of coins go through the mail, with minute losses if they are properly packed for mailing.

Right along with that are the people who have convinced themselves that the grading service is

Q: *I have a coin slabbed by ANACS when it was part of the ANA, giving the grade MS-63/65. Couldn't they make up their mind?*

A: *The right—or forward—slash (/) in this case gives separate grades for the obverse and the reverse. This usage is by no means universal. Some would use it to mean grades between 63 and 65. When determining value, it is best to use the lower grade. The right slash is also used to denote British pounds, overdates, doubled dates, doubled mintmarks, or calendar and regnal year separation.*

going to switch coins, or that a local coin dealer is going to switch the coin in a matter of seconds while examining it. As I pointed out elsewhere, the dealer is probably more worried that the customer is trying to pull a fast one.

The final chapter in this book is a condensed version of the *Official ANA Grading Standards for U.S. Coins*. It will give you a better idea of the way numerical grading works.

Q: *Please explain the "full bell lines" on the Franklin halves?*

A: *There are seven lines across the Liberty Bell, three near the rim and four more just above. A fully struck coin will show all seven lines without any interruption all the way across the bell. The concept was introduced before we got into numerical grading, which for the most part came before the "specialized" grading standards. However, there is still a core group that for one reason or another is not fully dependent on the numbers, that still use the full bell lines, full steps, split bands, full horn and other standards that had more to do with the strike in most cases.*

Chapter 34

INVESTING IN COINS

DON'T! If you are a beginning collector, even a moderately experienced collector, you are not ready to consider coins as an investment. I get dozens of questions every month about investing in coins. Many are greenhorns, with checkbook waving, expecting instant profits and a life of luxury. It does not work that way.

I tell them, "Become a collector. Spend 20 to 30 years collecting, until you have learned everything you can about coins. Then, consider whether to invest in coins."

Would you go blindly into the stock market without researching the company whose stock you want to buy? Would you, at a moment's notice, buy a carload of sow bellies? Why then would you think that investing in coins doesn't need any preparation? You can lose your shirt just as easily buying coins as you can buying sowbellies or a thousand shares of Shady Deal stock.

A common U.S. coin accumulation.

You will find plenty of TV pitchmen selling you coins. You will find telemarketers selling you coins. They and others pitch coins as the best investment going. Reread the line above - "You can lose your shirt ... "

But, don't go away mad. As you become a smart collector, you will find that many of the coins you already have are sporting a very nice premium. In the long term, coin prices as a group increase. Individual coins in that group can and do go down.

Does your crystal ball tell you which ones will do that? Mine doesn't. However, the questions roll in and the best answer I have is that my crystal ball is too cloudy to be of any help - and if it did help, I'd be using the knowledge to make myself rich. The hard facts are that there is no way to predict the coin market any more than you can predict how the stock market is going to do from day to day.

Some good pieces of advice should be repeated here. Collect what you like, not what someone tells you to collect, or the latest pitch on your TV. Beware of fire-sale prices. The overwhelming odds are that they will not be a bargain. Don't buy anything offered in a cold call from someone you don't know. Avail yourself of the benefits of having your phone number - and cell phone number - on the national "Do Not Call" list. However, don't forget that the rules exempt firms with which you have done business, so don't give them a head start.

Stack of gold bars

Investing in gold, platinum or silver bullion is entirely another matter. Precious metals go by different rules than the coins made from them. Consider this. When you buy gold, in the form of bars, you are entering a market that is dominated by the Central Banks of many of the major nations around the world. Your hundreds of dollars are matched against millions of dollars, even billions of dollars, worth of gold. You are taking on bankers with decades of experience and who can dump tons of gold on the market literally at a moment's notice.

Just as there are fake and altered coins, so, too, are there fake bullion bars. It may be a gold bar with the center hollowed out and filled with lead. It may be a solid block of lead with gold plating. This means that before you sell your bars, you may have to pay for an expensive assay. With bullion coins, this is not usually a problem.

Platinum markets are nearly as volatile and there is far less platinum than gold available. Currently platinum is selling for roughly twice the value of gold, but it wasn't that long ago that the two metals were neck and neck in price.

Silver brings with it a wholly different set of circumstances. It's much more plentiful than either gold or platinum. It was the key metal in the Hunt family's attempt to corner the metals market in 1980, when the price went to $52 an ounce.

As this is being written, silver is slightly above $7 an ounce. Thousands of investors are sitting on silver that they paid $8, $10, $15 or even $20 or more. Most of them will sell out if the price of silver ever gets back to what they paid. The deciding factor is India. Reliable reports indicate that there is enough silver buried in that country to meet demands for silver for several decades. If silver prices go up, that silver will be dug up again and will flatten the world market for the metal.

Last call. If you do decide against all advice to invest in gold, be absolutely certain that you are getting what you pay for. One of the biggest scams going is the company that offers to store your gold or gold coins while you are paying for them, and even after. Take possession of what you buy and store it in the safest possible place, with the keys in your possession. In the past, there have been dozens of companies pulling this scam, leaving investors with worthless receipts.

Q: *Do you offer the same advice to collectors and investors in coins?*

A: *For collectors my comments boil down to one simple piece of advice: collect what you like and enjoy. Advice for an investor is completely different, but often the two are confused. Granted, collectors often eye their collecting with an ultimate profit in mind, but the investor looks at coins strictly as a money making proposition. The investor is interested in the bottom line, not whether owning a particular coin, or set of coins, gives pleasure and enjoyment. Beyond advising potential investors to gain 20 to 30 years experience as a collector first, I don't give investment advice.*

Chapter 35

LEAVING YOUR COINS TO YOUR HEIRS

You are not too young to make a will. The odds of getting run over by a bus or having a heart attack at a tender age are slim, but these events do happen. Even for younger readers, it won't hurt to do some planning. If you don't plan, very bad things can happen. A lot of people don't want to talk about, or even think about their demise.

From personal experience, I can tell you that things go much smoother with advance plans in place.

Since you can't just toss your collection in the air to fall where it may, the best thing to do is will it to a friend - the guy you've swapped coins with for years. If that doesn't work, consider donating it to your local coin club, or to the ANA for a tax credit. The local club undoubtedly can use your reference library. If there are some rare and valuable books, donate them to the ANA. Don't will or give the collection or the books to a charity or church, as most have no facility to handle a collection and most likely will recover only a fraction of its real worth.

If, God forbid, your heirs are likely to get into a squabble over your estate, then designate exactly who you want to give or sell the coins to, or who should auction them off, so that the monetary proceeds can be divided according to your will. This is far better than trying to divide the coins equally. Expect a fight over your assets and you probably will be right. Forestall as much of the rancor as possible by leaving explicit instructions for the disposal of your collection.

Put your specific instructions with your collection. Give your lawyer or the potential executor of your estate copies and make them part of your will. Don't leave anything to chance and don't walk away muttering, "It's not my problem. Let them fight it out." Believe me, they will. Don't forget that list of the coins with the prices you paid for them. The IRS is waiting.

Chapter 36

BUYING & SELLING COINS

Here's where you get to put what you've learned from this book on the line.

1. *Buy the book before you buy - or sell - the coin.*

U.S. Coin Digest

2. *Know more about the coin than does the person selling it.*

3. *Know how to grade within a point.*

4. *Keep accurate records of every purchase and sale. The IRS is waiting.*

5. *Learn the minting process.*

A bin of coins coming from a coin press.

6. *Collect what you like and want, not what someone tells you to collect.*

7. *There are no dumb questions.*

8. *Don't be a checkbook collector.*

9. *Don't clean your coins.*

10. *Walk before you run.*

11. *Make a list.*

Coin price guides mostly quote retail prices for coins. This is because dealers use wholesale prices and add their individual markup, so no two dealers are likely to have the same retail prices. Coin dealers won't give you wholesale prices, but they may give a small discount if you look like a good customer.

When buying, use your senses. Look at the coin, preferably with a magnifier. Listen to what the dealer is saying about it. Since you already know a lot about the coin, you can compare the sales pitch with reality. Stop if the deal doesn't meet your criteria. In other words, "Stop, look and listen."

Coin Prices magazine

Q: *A safety deposit box, part of an estate, contained several hundred ancient coins. Local coin dealers showed no interest in them, offering only a few cents apiece. Aren't they worth more than that?*

A: *Chances are good that they are, but it's the same story, as with any other special area of the hobby, you need to contact a dealer who specializes in ancient coins. This is good advice for all collectors. Look for a dealer who specializes in the coins you are trying to sell (or buy). Numismatics is far too broad a field for any one person to be a specialist in every area. It's the same as your car. You wouldn't take a Mercedes to a Kia dealer, so use the same good judgment in picking a coin dealer. Best method—ask for a referral. Almost any dealer will know who among his or her fellow dealers is an expert on the coins you have.*

When you do find a dealer that meets your standards, hang on to him or her. The more business you do, the more you are likely to profit from buying. Most dealers are happy to share their expertise with regular customers.

Until you are expert in all areas of your collection, I would avoid buying "sight unseen" coins. This is the quickest way to the poor farm. Especially, wait until you have lots of experience before getting into Internet auctions. A seller's high rating doesn't necessarily mean you will get an accurately graded, problem-free coin.

Before buying that beautiful coin offered on TV, try the local coin dealers. In most cases, they can provide the same coin at a fraction of the cost.

When you sell, expect offers that are discounted heavily from the retail value, unless the coin is especially valuable, or one the dealer needs for a client. Many collectors make the mistake of expecting full retail from a dealer. Like any other business, the coin dealer has to buy at wholesale in order to profit on a retail sale, to pay the help, the rent, the taxes and other expenses of doing business.

Don't make the mistake of trying to sell your coins to other collectors by putting an ad in the paper. You are asking to get your coins hijacked, even if you meet your potential customers in a bank. It's unsafe at any speed. Most local coin clubs have swap meets or auctions where you are likely to do better and be in a safe environment.

Many "vest pocket" dealers offer coins for sale in the hobby publications classified sections, but I'll remind you that until you can grade for yourself, you need to be careful of the offers.

In the event you do have a problem with a classified or display ad seller, the publications have a person who serves as a consumer advocate, who can be of help in getting things straightened out. You will need every bit of the paper trail, a log of phone calls or e-mail messages and any other evidence that will be helpful, such as a listing by issue date and the page number of the ad you responded to. The more pertinent information you have, the more likely you will get a successful settlement.

When selling a collection, sell the coins as a group. Don't let anyone "cherry pick" the collection by buying the valuable coins and leaving the junk behind.

Make a list of your coins, showing exactly what you paid for each one. If you cannot show proof you paid a premium for a coin, the IRS will take the difference between the sale price and the face value of the coin as taxable profit. Picture what that does to a $20 gold piece. Copy this paragraph and post it where you can't miss it.

Q: *Explain spot plus ($0.00)*

A: *Dealer ads for silver or gold bullion bars frequently will quote a price in this manner. For example a 100-ounce silver bar might be offered at "Spot plus $0.35." This means that you would pay the (daily) spot silver price (currently about $7.00 an ounce) plus 35 cents an ounce, which is the dealer's charge to cover expense and any profit on the deal. Thus, a 100-ounce bar might cost 100 x $7.00 ($500) plus 100 x .35 ($35) or a total of $735. The spot price is the price paid "on the spot" for such metals as gold and silver. Because the price of the precious metals is constantly moving up and down, it is necessary to have a quote for "right now" for a sale, and this is the spot price.*

Q: *Where can I find a buyer for the Franklin Mint items that I have?*

A: *This is a question that is a regular in the mail, in email and on our telephone, with a number of questions coming from insurance agents who are trying to establish values before issuing a policy. The Franklin Mint frequently refers their callers to us because we issued a reference catalog of all of their products. However, the last catalog we issued was in 1982 and has long since gone out of print. Ironically there's a better market for the catalog than for some of the pieces listed in it. The products they put out are excellent, high quality material. However, they saturated the market with something that even in much smaller mintages would have to be held for 50 to 100 years or more before it would appreciate significantly. We stopped publishing a catalog simply because there was no real market and no prices we could quote that would mean anything. We do have both buy and sell classified sections for Franklin Mint material, so keep an eye on them.*

When selling, take your list and a few sample coins and shop them to several dealers to find the one with the most interest in your collection. If it is a large or valuable collection, you will want to find an appraiser to give you an idea of the value before you try to sell it. Here again, the list comes in handy.

Chapter 37

Dealers

I've mentioned coin dealers a number of times already, but they deserve a chapter of their own.

Coin dealers have had a bad rap. The public perception of coin dealers ranks them down close to used-car salesmen. This is an unfair assessment, due mainly to the fact that the public knows next to nothing about coin collecting. Their only contact probably was to try and sell some coins. Or they may have heard of a neighbor's "bad deal." Word of mouth is great advertising for a firm, but it can never catch up with bad-mouthing.

While there are a few bad apples in the bunch, the majority of coin dealers are like any retailer, hard-working assets to the community. Show me a

Coin dealers and customers at a bourse.

business that doesn't have some sinners, but the coin dealers continue to take it in the neck.

A big part of the problem is the misconception that coin dealers somehow differ from all other businesses that pay wholesale prices for the merchandise they sell at retail. Many collectors get furious when they are offered a discounted price for their coins. They display their ignorance of common business practices by this attitude and the result is unwarranted bad press for the dealer.

The solution is to realize that buying and selling coins is, in fact, a business and it will not survive if there is no profit. You, in turn, have several ways to ensure that you are not being ripped off.

It's a good idea when doing business with a dealer you are unfamiliar with to first make several small purchases. Questions to ask yourself include, "Was the dealer courteous? Did he know his stock? Was the coin accurately graded? Were you satisfied with the cost?" If the dealer passes the test, you've found a good place to do business on a larger scale. This is the same thing you would do when buying anything.

What's different between buying a coin or going into a hardware store and buying a pound of nails? Or going to a grocery store? Coin prices fluctuate. So does the price of grapes or bananas. The grocer buys from the producer at wholesale and sells at retail. Once you see the coin dealer as a business person, you will have come a long way toward a successful relationship with the dealer.

It will surprise you, but one of the biggest problems that dealers have is collectors trying to rip them off in any of a hundred ways, not limited to the thief who stuffs his pockets with coins when the dealer isn't looking or is taking care of a legitimate customer. That's one reason why you see heavy security at coin shows.

Coin dealers realize that they are prime targets not only for sneak thieves, but also for organized gangs that often trail a dealer leaving a show until he stops for gas or food. In a matter of seconds, the practiced robbers can break open car trunks, cut chains or break windows to get at coins inside the car, leaving the scene before the dealer even has a chance to react. As a result, dealers with high-end coins are turning to the armored car services to get them safely to and from a show.

If you are seen making big purchases at a show, the same thing could happen to you, so exercise more than the usual care to ensure you aren't being followed into the show and when you leave.

Show security is a major process. That's why you are required to wear a name badge while you are at the show. At a large show, there are multiples of millions of dollars in coins and paper money, so they naturally want to make sure the people prowling the floor are legitimate attendees. At large shows there will be an armed police officer at the door and others stationed around the room, along with plainclothes officers or guards roaming the floor. Remember, they are there for your protection.

One last piece of advice. If there is a disturbance on the show floor, don't rush over to gawk. If a shot were fired, you could easily be the accidental target. You won't see them, but a number of coin dealers provide their own protection with a gun close at hand. Don't let your natural curiosity get you into a bad situation.

When you've been to a dealer's shop or a show and purchased coins, don't leave them on the seat of your car. The best place is in the trunk until you get to the bank where you keep your coins or some other safe place. Always be alert to anyone near you as you approach your car. Hit the door-lock switch as you enter the car to foil a carjacker. Be security conscious at all times.

Chapter 38

JOIN A COIN CLUB

No matter what level you are at - novice, intermediate, expert or veteran - you will be well served if you join a coin club. If there isn't one in your city, then start one! The American Numismatic Association has free literature on starting a club, including a sample set of by-laws and a Constitution. All you have to do is ask.

A club meeting

Local coin clubs are really the backbone of the hobby. This is where the novice begins to learn from other members or from educational show and tell exhibits. Most clubs have a speaker putting on a program. If you are worried about security, so are the other members, so you have a common problem, but one that will not leave the room. Think security at all times.

Coin clubs are found at local, state, regional, national and international levels. Each has its own purpose. The state and regional clubs often have local clubs as members, with the locals sharing the information and expertise of the higher club.

Many of the regional and national clubs are specialist clubs, devoted to one particular portion of the hobby, such as the Token and Medal Society (TAMS), the Civil War Token Society (CWTS) or the Combined Organization of Numismatic Error Collectors of America (CONECA).

At the top of the international list is the 32,000-member American Numismatic Association, which has been around since 1891. Even older is the American Numismatic Society.

The ANA is chartered by Congress and has more than 500 local, regional and national clubs as members. Their mantra is education and they have a wide range of educational services, including the ever-expanding Summer Seminars and the new Coins in the Classroom program for teachers, as well as the largest numismatic museum and largest numismatic library in the country. I'm proud to have served on the ANA Board of Governors.

If there's a numismatic collectible, there's probably a club devoted to it. If you are on the Internet, you can reach the ANA list of member clubs at www.money.org. Many of the clubs have their own Web sites.

For the beginning collector, I strongly urge you to join a local club, with an eye on joining the

ANA and any regional or national club that matches your collecting interests. Dues for most clubs are quite reasonable. One of the better examples is the Mesa Coin Club in Arizona, which offers a life membership for $5 as long as you attend at least one meeting in a calendar year.

A suggestion I've been making in programs I've done recently for local clubs is to start a mentoring program. List each club member's specialties. When a new member comes in, assign him or her to the club member with the same or similar specialties as a mentor. The new member has a lot to learn and the specialists have a lot of knowledge they can share.

You may get a negative reaction from some of the club members, especially those that avoid any work. However, the point to bring across is that every collector is a specialist at some level. Literally anyone who knows two facts is way ahead of the one-fact person and miles ahead of the no-fact person. That's why your club members are considered to be specialists.

It's far better in a one-on-one situation, but I've been mentoring collectors by mail and e-mail for many years. I've read almost all of the books in my reference library, so I'm classed as an expert in several areas. My question-and-answer columns have reached many thousands of collectors with new knowledge and my books are reaching thousands more. You don't have to be a successful author to be a mentor, but it helps.

Chapter 39

RESOURCES TO HELP YOU COLLECT

This is one of those "Where to Start?" chapters. There are literally hundreds of resources available. One already mentioned is the ANA's Dwight Manley Library, which with more than 50,000 books, is the largest numismatic library in the country. ANA, not so incidentally, is the largest numismatic organization in the world.

The nice thing is that it is a lending library, so ANA members can borrow almost any book just by paying the postage. Non-members can also borrow books, but they have to go through the inter-library system at their local library. The ANA library also fields research questions, but be warned that there is a $35-an-hour fee for extensive research.

There are lots of publications. F+W Publications has no less than five separate magazines and newspapers - *Coins Magazine, Coin Prices Magazine, Numismatic News* (the oldest coin hobby publication), *World Coin News* and *Bank Note Reporter*. My "Clinic" columns appear in all but Coin Prices magazine. In addition, there are numerous price guides, books and catalogs covering the broad spectrum of numismatics. You can find them - with excerpts - on the Internet at www.collect.com.

Several other publishers offer competing books, magazines and newspapers. It undoubtedly will surprise even some of the old timers to learn that there is a substantial amount of competition in the hobby publishing business. Price guides are a typical example. Protecting a heavy investment in pricing information is a constant struggle, especially when someone comes along and says, "Why don't you get your prices from (another publication)?" Not only would it be a copyright violation, but since there is a legion of specialists providing us with pricing information, we believe we have more accurate pricing information.

Evidence of the lack of comprehension is the next guy that comes along and says, "Your price is way off from so-and-so, so you need to correct it." Once someone has convinced themselves of the "truth," no amount of arguing is going to help point out that just perhaps so-and-so is wrong and not us.

A number of coin dealers also send out publications ranging from flyers to multi-page magazines. Many of the coin clubs have monthly or quarterly publications. Back to the ANA, which publishes the monthly *Numismatist* as a membership benefit, with articles on a wide array of numismatic topics, and offers collecting supplies in its Money Market. Most auction houses also issue color catalogs for their sales.

Coin price guides come in all hues. F+W Publications contributes *North American Coins and Prices*, which lists Canadian and Mexican coins besides the U.S. coins. It also has a dozen chapters devoted to all phases of coin collecting.

This list could go on and on, but with limited space we need to aim you in the right direction to find answers for yourself. I answer up to a dozen questions a day on the Internet and there are several clubs and commercial sources that you can find on the Internet.

Learn how to use one of the search engines on the Internet. It's relatively easy and you'll be amazed at the amount of information you can find. If you use the advanced section of Google, you'll no doubt be astounded by the speed with which hundreds or even thousands of pages related to your topic are found.

A popular newsgroup is rec.collecting.coins, and the matching rec.collecting.paper-money. Questions asked on either newsgroup are often answered in a matter of minutes. Just watch out for the jokers who like to see their names in print.

Ask lots of questions. I'll be glad to answer them, or refer you to one of the specialists in that particular area. You can reach me on the Internet at AnswerMan2@aol.com. My mailing address is:

Alan Herbert
F+W Publications
700 E. State St.
Iola, WI 54990-0001

Chapter 40

YOUR COIN COLLECTING LIBRARY

Do I need to repeat "Buy the book" … ?

Your numismatic library can be as large or small as you choose. If you are a typical collector, you may have a price guide and perhaps one or two other books. If you are a smart collector, you will have at least one bookcase shelf full.

You will need as a minimum, the following:

1. *An up-to-date price guide.*

2. *A grading guide.*

3. *A detailed explanation of the minting process.*

4. *A subscription to one or more of the hobby publications.*

5. *A specialty club membership that includes a publication.*

6. *Any available books on your specialty or collecting interest.*

7. *A numismatic dictionary or encyclopedia.*

I'm not suggesting that you get all of them

immediately, but I do recommend that you budget for their purchase, along with the tools and coins that you are collecting. You can establish your own priorities as to when you acquire them.

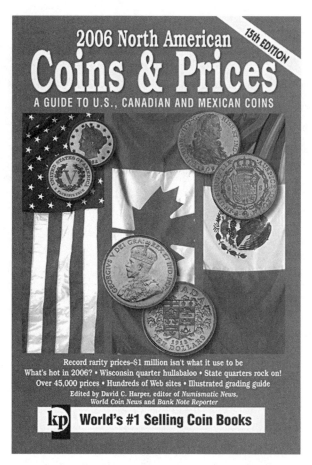

A common reference work

As your library grows, you will undoubtedly add reference material from other areas of the hobby. There will be new books published that you will want. It's a hard choice to make, deciding whether to buy a book or a coin, but the benefits of the book will be long term.

Be sure that when you work out your hobby budget for the year, you include money for subscriptions, club dues, tools and supplies, and reference books, along with your coins. The four expenditures will give you the largest possible return and the biggest bang for your buck. Once you begin to understand the benefits, you will realize that you actually are investing in knowledge. Once you have the knowledge, it will earn dividends with every coin you add to your collection.

By now you more fully realize the complexities of the coin hobby. I've been able to barely scratch the surface, but there are tons of information and advice out there waiting for you to come along. It takes work, but there is satisfaction at the end of the tunnel that you probably couldn't find in any other way.

Q: *What is Territorial Gold?*

A: *This was the name applied to privately issued gold from territories, which later became part of the United States, most notably from California.*

Chapter 41

YOUR NUMISMATIC GLOSSARY

Way back at the beginning of this book, I mentioned the secret language of the coin collector. While I can't list all the terms and abbreviations, I've tried to list the most common ones. As you progress in the hobby you will find other terms and you will find other sources for their definitions.

First, a few common abbreviations:

AG - About Good. Verbal coin grade.

Ag - Symbol for Silver

AGW - Actual Gold Weight in a coin

APW - Actual Platinum Weight in a coin.

ASW - Actual Silver Weight in a coin

AU - About Uncirculated. Adjectival coin grade.

BU - Brilliant Uncirculated. Adjectival coin grade.

CAM, DCAM - Cameo, Deep Cameo

COA - Certificate of Authenticity

Cu - Symbol for copper.

Cu-Ni - Symbol for copper-nickel alloy

- - (Dash) In a chart, means no figure available, especially mintage figures.

DMPL - Deep Mirror Proof-like

Dwt - Pennyweight

EF - (or XF) - Extra Fine. Adjectival coin grade.

F - Fine. Adjectival coin grade.

Fe - Symbol for iron

FPL - Fixed Price List

G - Good. Adjectival coin grade.

I.A., I.B. - (or Inc. Abv., Inc. Bel.-
   Included Above or Included Below.
   (Mintages of two or more varieties, or
   two or more years bulked together.)

MM - Mintmark

MS - Mint State, or uncirculated. With
   a number (MS-60), a numerical
   grade.

Ni - Symbol for nickel.

OMM - Overmintmark. One letter over a
   different letter.

PL – Proof-like.

PVC   Polyvinyl Chloride

SASE – Self-Addressed Stamped Envelope

SMS - Special Mint Set (1965-1967)

*A "D" mintmark
from the Denver
Mint.*

V.D.B. initials on the reverse of a 1909 Lincoln cent.

S-VDB - 1909-S cent with Victor David
   Brenner's initials

TF - Tail Feathers, as 8TF on 1878 Morgan
   dollars.

An 1878 Morgan dollar with eight tail feathers on the eagle.

Unc. - Uncirculated. Adjectival coin grade.

VF - Very Fine. Adjectival coin grade.

VG - Very Good. Adjectival coin grade.

XF - (or EF) - Extra Fine. Adjectival coin grade.

Zn - Symbol for zinc

Then come a few of the many numismatic terms. These and the preceding abbreviations are adapted from the forthcoming American Numismatic Association Numismatic Dictionary:

Abrasion - Marks caused by friction or rubbing as a form of wear, as differing from bag marks or hairlines. Usually found on the high points of the design and not as deep or obvious as a contact mark.

Acid Date - A date, especially on a Buffalo nickel, made readable by applying acid to the coin. An alteration.

Alloy - 1. A mixture of two or more metals, melted and mixed together.

2. Referring to any metal or combination of metals mixed with bullion. Usually copper.

Alteration - Any deliberate change, such as the addition, removal or reworking of any design element on a coin, whether to deceive, confuse or to promote a cause.

Average Circulated - Coin dealer term for a group of coins that generally grade at the low end of the grading scale, but for which there are no actual standards.

Bourse - A hall or venue where dealers set up tables to display and buy and sell coins and other numismatic objects. From the French term for exchange.

A "hobo" nickel, carved out of the Indian head on a Buffalo nickel.

Chop Mark - Marks applied in the Orient to coins, indicating that they are full weight and the correct fineness. Found especially on Mexican and U.S. Trade dollars.

A chop-marked coin

Coin - A piece issued or sanctioned by a governmental body, with an assigned or stated commercial value.

Coin Board - An open-face album, without a cover, usually with folds so that the outside protects the contents. Has holes for a given series or group of coins.

Collector Value - The value above face value attached to a given coin because of its date, mintmark and grade.

A coin with a large major die break. A "cud."

Cud - Slang - A fictional term for a major die break, so called because of the appearance of the raised metal as being similar to a "cud" of chewing gum or tobacco resting on the coin.

Face Value - The value of a coin as stated on the piece.

Incuse - The opposite of relief. A design that is sunk into the face of the coin or into the face of a die.

Key Coin - A coin that is one of the rarer grades, dates or mints for a given series.

Legend - The principal wording or phrase on a coin.

The 1983 and 1984 Olympic Commemorative dollars had incuse dates.

A 1968-S cent with very widespread machine doubling damage.

Machine Doubling Damage (MDD) - Damage to a struck coin caused by one of the dies bouncing or chattering on the surface. The root cause is loose or worn parts of the machinery that allow slack that lets the die move about. The resulting doubling is often confused with hub doubling. Since this occurs after the final impact of the die pair, it is damage and reduces, rather than increases, collector value. Commonly mislabeled as strike doubling, shift, shift doubling or micro-doubling.

Medal - A piece issued either by a government or a private entity intended to honor or memorialize a person, event, location or other worthy subject. Medals do not have a stated monetary value and are not intended for commerce. Often mislabeled as coins.

Minting Variety - A coin that is normal or exhibits a variation from the normal, as a result of any portion of the minting process, whether at the planchet stage, as a result of a change or modification of the die or during the striking process. It includes those classes considered to be intentional changes, as well as those caused by normal wear and tear on the dies or other minting equipment, and classes deemed to be "errors."

Novelty Coin - Any coin that has been altered in some fashion after leaving the mint, including, but not limited to, cents with Lincoln smoking a pipe or cigar, with Kennedy's bust, with

A novelty coin with added design.

state maps, fraternal order symbols, etc. Technically an altered coin, but with minor collector value.

Overdate - Any date that has a second date with one or more differing digits superimposed by a doubled hub or by the use of punches or engraving tools on the die.

A 1943/1942-P nickel overdate

Packaging Mistake - A mint-packaged proof or mint set that has a missing coin, duplicate coins, two coins in one hole or partition or any other mistake.

Planchet - The processed disc (usually metal) that is placed between the die pair to be struck as a coin.

Proof-like - A coin that exhibits some, but not all of the characteristics of a proof coin, such as mirror fields, sharp strike (two or more), frosted devices, etc.

Ringing an Auction - Collusion between several buyers eliminating competition by agreeing in advance on what items they will bid for.

Ring Test - A negative test involving dropping the coin on a hard surface to determine the metal content by the sound, or "ring" of the coin. The smallest internal defect or void will cause a perfectly good bullion coin to sound like a block of lead.

Sea Salvaged - Term used to describe coins recovered from ocean wrecks. The coins usually show damage from long contact with salt water or with the sand, affecting silver coins more than the gold. Also water damaged.

Shotgun Roll - Slang - A paper roll with both ends crimped, similar to the end of a shotgun shell, hence the name. The method of rolling exposes most of the two end coins.

Slab, Slabbing, Slabbed - Slang - A hard plastic case used by a third-party grading service to encapsulate a coin that has been graded and authenticated.

Coins in plastic slabs.

Token - A privately issued piece, usually with an assigned value intended for use similar to a coin.

Troy Weight - A system of weights used primarily for bullion, in that 12 troy ounces equal one troy pound, or 5,760 grains. A troy ounce equals 480 grains or 31.103 grams. (See Avoirdupois Weight)

TRVST - The spelling of TRUST on all Peace dollars and Standing Liberty quarters. The cause is blamed on artistic license based on the lack of a U in the Roman alphabet.

TRVST on a Peace dollar

Whiz, Whizzing - To alter the surface of a coin by removing or moving the surface metal about. A practice condemned by the ANA and the Professional Numismatist's Guild.

Wooden Money - Properly they are tokens, printed on pieces of wood. The first was on thin slices of wood. Later rounds similar to coins also were used. Some medals are found that are actually struck on wood.

A typical piece of wooden money.

Chapter 42

GOING TO A COIN SHOW

A typical coin "bourse."

If you are fortunate enough to live in or near a city, there is likely to be a coin show nearby. Reader surveys at F+W indicate that the average collector is willing to drive up to 200 miles to get to a show. Really serious collectors might drive several hundred miles beyond that or fly to a distant show.

What's the attraction? That's a question with several answers. The biggest selling point is the opportunity to find a large group of coin dealers in one spot. It's as if your favorite mall had every hardware store in the city side by side. Say you collect Indian Head cents. There might be 10 or a dozen dealers who specialize in them. Can you hear opportunity knocking?

It's also a chance to meet and talk to other collectors, at least some of whom are probably interested in collecting the same things you are. At the larger shows there will be exhibits to learn from, club meetings, educational programs and even experts who can appraise or grade your coins.

Before you go, there are some things you need to know. Your first coin show is going to be a revelation in a lot of ways. If you know the rules beforehand, you will turn it into an exciting leap forward in the hobby.

Before you go, make sure the show is going on as scheduled. Information about shows often is published months in advance. In the meantime, the show may have been postponed, moved or even cancelled. Nothing is more upsetting than driving to a coin show only to find an empty building. Even the big shows sometimes have problems. For example, the 2005 ANA World's Fair of Money, the largest coin show in the world, had to be moved at the last minute from San Jose to San Francisco. The bigger shows will spread the word of any changes, but the smaller shows may not, so check ahead.

If you are planning on a distant show where you will be spending more than one day, most promoters will have a block of rooms at a nearby hotel at reduced rates. Find out and make reservations well in advance.

It's a good idea to take along a checklist of the coins you are looking for. Don't forget to bring a bag. A heavy cloth shopping bag is a good starter. Later, you may want to get an aluminum case - like a small suitcase - or an attaché case to carry your coins. Vest-pocket dealers frequently use small, wheeled carry-on bags to carry their stock.

At many shows, there will be publications and other literature that will go in the bag so they don't get laid down and forgotten in the excitement of the chase. A price guide is also helpful, as is a notebook to keep track of your purchases and sales. You need to keep track for the IRS, as well as for your own records.

You arrive at the front door of the show. Now what? Keep your wits about you as you look around. There are coins everywhere! At a small show, there may be only 20 to 30 dealers. At a large show, such as the Florida FUN Show, or the ANA World's Fair, there may be up to 500 or more dealers.

Depending on who is putting on the show, there will be a registration at the door, perhaps even a fee or an expected donation, or there may be an opportunity to participate in a door prize drawing.

Entrance to a show is based on security. There are millions of dollars worth of coins on the dealer's tables, which they and the armed guards have to protect. You will probably need to wear a name badge while you are in the show. If you try to walk in without one, you will be promptly sent back to get one.

The room where the dealers are set up is known as the "bourse" floor, a fancy French term for a room full of dealers. Everyone who comes to the show will follow their personal pattern, whether it's to stop at the first table, turn left, turn right, or circle the room to see what's there before starting to seriously look at coins.

Here's where some rules come into play. Don't walk up to a table and interrupt a transaction that is already going on. Wait your turn.

Ask, if you don't see the coin you are looking for on display, but remember, dealers specialize just like collectors, so you needn't bother to ask for a U.S. coin at a dealer's table with just a display of Roman coins.

Don't ever bring food or a drink with you to a dealer's table. Don't lay your bag (or anything else) on the glass display cases. Besides the danger of breakage, you are hiding the dealer's stock from the next customer, in effect showing disrespect for the dealer's stock. A spilled drink can do many thousands of dollars in damage that you could be liable for. The dealer may or may not caution you, but you can avoid embarrassment by closely following this advice.

If you are looking at several coins, or a box full, keep both hands (and the coins) above the table at all times. Don't mix your coins with the dealer's coins. The dealer is watching you because you just might be one of the thieves that show up at a lot of shows.

Keep the conversation at a minimum, unless the dealer encourages it. A gushing and overly detailed description of every last coin in your collection is going to turn off the most patient of dealers. If you are the only customer, it's safe to ask questions, but as soon as another customer approaches, break it off.

Stay out of any deals going on around you.

Repeat: stay out. Don't pipe up and announce that there's a better example of the coin in another aisle or show one from your collection. Don't offer advice and don't try to outbid another buyer. Any kind of interference that might spoil a sale is going to get the dealer very angry, with good reason, so stay out.

Don't expect, or ask, for a "dealer" discount. A couple of questions will expose the fact that you are lying. A dealer may give you a smaller discount, depending on the number of coins or value that you are buying. It doesn't hurt to dicker, but your success will vary from dealer to dealer, the time of day or how business is going.

Take time to look at the exhibits. There is a tremendous amount of knowledge in a compact space that you can learn from. Spend some time at any book dealer's table, looking for books on your specialty. Remember, this is not a reading room or a library. Treat any book with care, especially softcover books that will bend or fold easily. Both hard- and softcover books can suffer permanent damage if you open them too wide and break the back. Don't handle or touch books that you are not seriously interested in. Resist that temptation to "feel."

Another don't has some ifs involved - it's usually never a good idea to spend all your money at one table. You may find a better example or a higher grade at another table, so sit firmly on your checkbook until you decide which is the best deal. Having so many dealers gives you a much wider selection than what an individual dealer has to offer.

Q: *Exactly what does a "bust" mean? Is it the full figure?*

A: *A bust is defined as the head, neck and upper trunk of a person's body. Webster describes it as "head and shoulders."*

Remember, dealers who offer coins for sale also buy coins. They have to, to stay in business. You may see only one or two "We Buy" signs, but if you have coins you want to sell, virtually every dealer whose specialty covers your coins will usually be ready to buy. Again, you can move from table to table for the best offer.

If a dealer turns his back to you, won't get his nose out of the newspaper, fails to greet you or ignores you in other ways, move on. He or she doesn't want your business and certainly won't offer you any bargains. If it were the only game in town you would be stuck with it, but at a coin show you have more options.

It all boils down to respect. If you treat a dealer and his stock in trade with respect, the dealer will treat you with the same respect. If not, move on to another table. That's one of the nice things about a coin show. You have other chances to make a successful buy that will make your day.

For your first show, I'd recommend a lot of looking and not much buying. You are there to learn, rather than to collect. Watch how other collectors go about looking for their coins. Watch the dealers in action. As you get more shows under your belt, you will have a better idea of what's going on and how to spot any bargains that might tempt you. If you stick to the rules, things will go much easier for you and you will be able to more fully enjoy your visit to the bourse floor.

Select U.S. Numismatic Events

F.U.N. — *Florida United Numismatists Annual Convention: Early-January • Orlando, Florida*

NYINC — *New York International Coin Convention: Mid-January • Manhattan, New York*

Long Beach Coin Expo —*Three Annual Shows • February, June & September • Long Beach, California*

CPMX — *Chicago Paper Money Expo: March • Chicago*

Bay State Coin Show— *Two Annual Shows • March & November • Boston*

Baltimore Coin and Currency Convention— *Three Annual Shows • March, July & December • Baltimore*

Atlantique City — *Giant "all antiques" event, including coins & paper money: Two Annual Events • March & October • Atlantic City, New Jersey*

Santa Clara Coin, Stamp & Collectibles Expo — *Two Annual Shows • March & November • Santa Clara, California*

CICF — *Chicago International Coin Fair: March-April • Chicago*

ANA — *American Numismatic Association - Spring Convention: April 7-9, 2006 • Atlanta March 23-25, 2007 • Sacramento, California March 7-9, 2008 • Phoenix*

CSNS — *Central States Numismatic Society Annual Convention: April 26-29, 2006 • Columbus, Ohio (check the website, www.centralstates.info, for future show locations and dates)*

GSNA — *Garden State Numismatic Convention: May • New Jersey*

Denver Coin Expo— *May & September • Denver*

Memphis Paper Money Show— *June • Memphis, Tennessee*

MidAmerica Coin Expo— *June • Chicago*

ANA — *American Numismatic Association- World's Fair of Money: Aug. 16-19, 2006 • Denver Aug. 8-12, 2007 • Milwaukee July 30-Aug. 3, 2008 • Baltimore*

PCDA — *Professional Currency Dealers Association National Convention: November • St. Louis*

MSNS — *Michigan State Numismatic Society Fall Convention: November (Thanksgiving weekend) • Dearborn, Michigan*

Chapter 43

THE ANA GRADING GUIDE

With permission from the American Numismatic Association, I am including an excerpt from the official *ANA Grading Guide* to help you to better understand the grading terms and their meaning. A basic understanding of how to grade your coins is vital to your collecting interests at any level.

Grades listed are based on the following standards established by the American Numismatic Association. For more detailed descriptions, see the *Official ANA Grading Standards for United States Coins* by Ken Bressett and A. Kosoff (American Numismatic Association, 818 N. Cascade Ave., Colorado Springs, CO 80903-3279).

Proof coins. The term "proof" refers to a manufacturing process that results in a special surface or finish on coins made for collectors. Most familiar are modern brilliant proofs. These coins are struck at the U.S. Mint by a special process. Carefully prepared dies, sharp in all features, are made. Then the flat surfaces of the dies are given a high, mirror-like polish. Specially prepared planchets are fed into low-speed coining presses. Each proof coin is slowly and carefully struck more than once to accentuate details. When striking is completed, the coin is taken from the dies with care and not allowed to come into contact with other pieces. The result is a coin with a mirror-like surface. The piece is then grouped together with other denominations in a set and offered for sale to collectors.

From 1817 through 1857, proof coins were made only on special occasions and not for general sale to collectors. They were made available to visiting foreign dignitaries, government officials and those with connections at the Mint. Earlier (pre-1817) U.S. coins may have proof-like surfaces and many proof characteristics (1796 silver coins are good examples), but they were not specifically or intentionally struck as proofs. These are sometimes designated as "specimen strikings."

Beginning in 1858, proofs were sold to collectors openly. In that year, 80 silver proof sets (containing silver coins from the three-cent through the dollar), plus additional pieces of the silver-dollar denomination were produced, as well as perhaps 200 (the exact number is not known) copper-nickel cents and a limited number of proof gold coins.

The traditional, or "brilliant," type of proof finish was used on all American proof coins of the 19th century. During the 20th century, cents through the 1909 Indian type, nickels through the 1912 Liberty, regular-issue silver coins through 1915 and gold coins through 1907 were of the brilliant type. When modern proof coinage was resumed in 1936 and continued through 1942, then 1950-1964, and 1968 to date, the brilliant finish was used. These types of proofs are referred to as "brilliant proofs," although actual specimens may have toned over the years. The mirror-like surface is still evident, however.

From 1908 through 1915, matte proofs and sandblast proofs (the latter made by directing fine sand particles at high pressure toward the coin's surface) were made of certain coins (exceptions are the 1909-1910 proofs with Roman finish). Characteristics vary from issue to issue, but generally all of these pieces have extreme sharpness of design detail and sharp, squared-off rims. The surfaces are without luster and have a dullish matte surface. Sandblasted proofs were made of certain commemoratives also, such as the 1928 Hawaiian issue.

Roman-finish proof gold coins were made in 1909 and 1910. These pieces are sharply struck and have squared-off edges and a satin-like surface finish, not too much different from an uncirculated coin (which causes confusion among collectors today and which, at the time of issue, was quite unpopular because collectors resented having to pay a premium for a coin without a distinctly different appearance).

Matte proofs were made of 1908-1917 Lincoln cents and 1913-1917 Buffalo nickels. Such coins have extremely sharp design detail, squared-off rims, and "brilliant" (mirror-like) edges, but a matte or satin-like (or even satin surface, not with flashy mint luster) surface. In some instances, matte-proof dies may have been used to make regular circulation strikes once the requisite number of matte proofs was made for collectors. So it is important that a matte proof, to be considered authentic, have squared-off rims and mirror-like perfect edges in addition to the proper surface characteristics.

Additional points concerning proofs. Certain regular issues, or business strikes, have nearly full proof-like surfaces. These were produced in several ways. Usually regular-issue dies (intended to make coins for circulation) were polished to remove surface marks or defects for extended use. Coins struck from these dies were produced at high speed, and the full proof surface is not always evident. Also, the pieces are struck on ordinary planchets. Usually such pieces, sometimes called "first strikes" or "proof-like uncirculated," have patches of uncirculated mint frost. A characteristic in this regard is the shield on the reverse (on coins with this design feature). The stripes within the shield on proofs are fully brilliant, but on proof-like non-proofs the stripes usually are not mirror-like. Also, the striking may be weak in areas and the rims might not be sharp.

The mirror-like surface of a brilliant proof coin is much more susceptible to damage than the surfaces of an uncirculated coin. For this reason, proof coins that have been cleaned often show a series of fine hairlines or minute striations. Also, careless handling has resulted in certain proofs acquiring marks, nicks and scratches.

Some proofs, particularly 19th-century issues, have "lint marks." When a proof die was wiped with an oily rag, sometimes threads, bits of hair, lint and so on would remain. When a coin was struck from such a die, an incuse or recess impression of the debris would appear on the piece. Lint marks visible to the unaided eye should be specially mentioned in a description.

Proofs are divided into the following classifications:

Proof-70— *A Proof-70, or "perfect proof," has no hairlines, handling marks or other defects; in other words, a flawless coin. Such a coin may be brilliant or may have natural toning.*

Proof-67— *A grade midway between Proof-70 and Proof-65 and would be noticeably finer than Proof-65.*

Proof-65— *Proof-65, or "choice proof," refers to a proof that may show some very fine hairlines, usually from friction-type cleaning or friction-type drying or rubbing after dipping. To the unaided eye, a Proof-65 will appear to be virtually perfect. However, 4X magnification will reveal some minute lines. Such hairlines are best seen under strong incandescent light.*

Proof-63— *A coin midway between Proof-65 and Proof-60.*

Proof-60— *A coin with some scattered handling marks and hairlines visible to the unaided eye.*

Impaired proofs; other comments. If a proof has been excessively cleaned, has many marks, scratches, dents or other defects, it is described as an impaired proof. If the coin has seen extensive wear, then it will be graded one of the lesser grades: Proof-55, Proof-45, and so on. It is not logical to describe a slightly worn proof as "AU" ("almost uncirculated) for it never was "uncirculated" in the sense that "uncirculated" describes a top-grade, normal-production strike. So the term "impaired proof" is appropriate. It is best to describe fully such a coin. Examples: "Proof with extensive hairlines and scuffing." "Proof with numerous nicks and scratches in the field." "Proof-55, with light wear on the higher surfaces."

Uncirculated coins.

The term "uncirculated," interchangeable with "mint state," refers to a coin that has never seen circulation. Such a piece has no wear of any kind. A coin as bright as the time it was minted or with very light natural toning can be described as "toned uncirculated." Except for copper coins, the presence or absence of light toning does not affect an uncirculated coin's grade. Indeed, among silver coins, attractive natural toning often results in the coin bringing a premium.

The quality of luster or "mint bloom" on an uncirculated coin is an essential element in correctly grading the piece and has a bearing on its value. Luster may in time become dull, frosty, spotted, or discolored. Unattractive luster will normally lower the grade.

Except for certain special mint sets made in recent years for collectors, uncirculated, or normal production-strike coins, were produced on high-speed presses, stored in bags together with other coins, run through counting machines, and in other ways handled without regard to numismatic posterity. As a result, it is the rule and not the exception for an uncirculated coin to have bag marks and evidence of coin-to-coin contact, although the piece might not have seen actual commercial circulation. The number of such marks will depend on the coin's size. Differences in criteria in this regard are given in the individual sections under grading descriptions for different denominations and types.

Uncirculated coins can be divided into five major categories:

MS-70— MS-70, or perfect uncirculated, is the finest quality available. Such a coin under 4X magnification will show no bag marks, lines, or other evidence of handling or contact with other coins.

A brilliant coin may be described as "MS-70 brilliant" or "perfect brilliant uncirculated." A lightly toned nickel or silver coin may be described as "MS-70 toned" or "perfect toned uncirculated." Or, in the cases of particularly attractive or unusual toning, additional adjectives may be in order such as "perfect uncirculated with attractive iridescent toning around the borders."

Copper and bronze coins: To qualify as MS-70, a copper or bronze coin must have its full luster and natural surface color, and may not be toned brown, olive, or any other color. Coins with toned surfaces that are otherwise perfect should be described as MS-65, rather than MS-67.

MS-67— *This refers to a coin that is midway between MS-70 and MS-65. The coin may be either brilliant or toned (except for a copper coin, for which a toned piece should be described as MS-65).*

MS-65— *This refers to an above uncirculated coin that may be brilliant or toned (and described* accordingly) and that has fewer bag marks than usual; scattered, occasional bag marks on the surface or perhaps one or two very light rim marks.

MS-63— *A coin midway between MS-65 and MS-60.*

MS-60— *MS-60, or uncirculated (typical uncirculated without any other adjectives) refers to a coin that has a moderate number of bag marks on its surface. Also present may be a few minor edge nicks and marks, although not of a serious nature. Unusually deep bag marks, nicks and the like must be described separately. A coin may be either brilliant or toned.*

The numerical grades, along with their prevailing adjectival grades and descriptions, are as follows:

MS-63— *(choice uncirculated): choice quality specimens with minimal weaknesses or blemish readily evident.*

MS-64— *choice quality specimens with eye appeal and only the smallest distracting weakness, blemish or bag marks.*

MS-65— *(gem uncirculated): sharply struck, hairline-free coins with full luster and no distracting blemishes.*

MS-67— *described as "gem" according to official ANA criteria, it is not presently associated with an adjectival equivalent. There is also not a consensus description that is associated with this grade.*

Striking and mint peculiarities on uncirculated coins. Certain early U.S. gold and silver coins have mint-caused planchet or adjustment marks, a series of parallel striations. If these are visible to the naked eye, they should be described adjectively in addition to the numerical or regular descriptive grade. For example: "MS-60 with adjustment marks," or "MS-65 with adjustment marks," or "perfect uncirculated with very light adjustment marks," or something similar.

If an uncirculated coin exhibits weakness due to striking or die wear, or unusual (for the variety) die wear, this must be adjectively mentioned in addition to the grade. Examples are "MS-60 lightly struck" or "choice uncirculated, lightly struck," and "MS-70, lightly struck."

Circulated coins. Once a coin enters circulation, it begins to show signs of wear. As time goes on, the coin becomes more and more worn until, after a period of many decades, only a few features may be left.

Dr. William H. Sheldon devised a numerical scale to indicate degrees of wear. According to this scale, a coin in condition 1, or "basal state," is barely recognizable. At the opposite end, a coin touched by even the slightest trace of wear (below MS-60) cannot be called uncirculated.

Although numbers from 1 through 59 are continuous, it has been found practical to designate specific intermediate numbers to define grades. Hence, this text uses the following descriptions and their numerical equivalents:

About Uncirculated

AU-50 (about uncirculated)—*Just a slight amount of wear from brief exposure to circulation or light rubbing from mishandling may be found on the elevated design areas. Those imperfections may appear as scratches or dull spots, along with bag marks or edge nicks. At least half of the original mint luster will usually be present.*

Indian Cent

Lincoln Cent

Buffalo Nickel

Jefferson Nickel

Mercury Dime

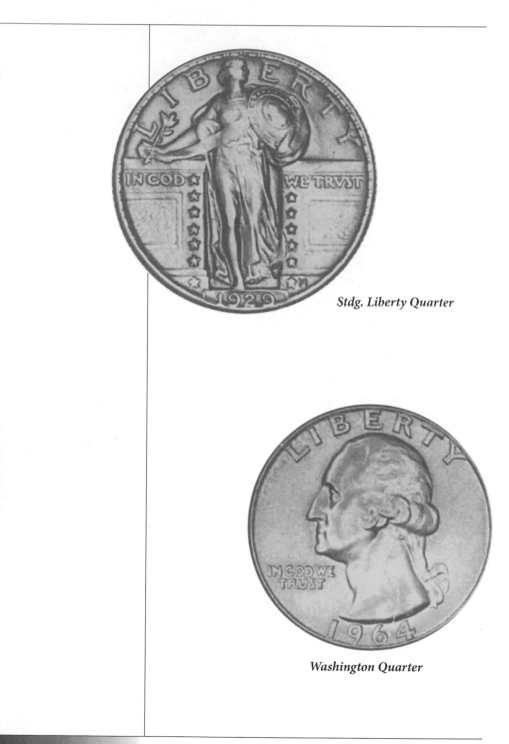

Stdg. Liberty Quarter

Washington Quarter

Wlkg. Liberty Half

Morgan Dollar

Barber Coins

Extremely Fine

EF-40 (extremely fine)—*Coins must show only slight evidence of wear on the highest points of the design, particularly in the hair lines of the portrait on the obverse and the eagle's feathers and wreath found on most U.S. coins. A trace of mint luster may show in protected areas of the coin's surface.*

Indian Cent

Lincoln Cent

Buffalo Nickel

Jefferson Nickel

Mercury Dime

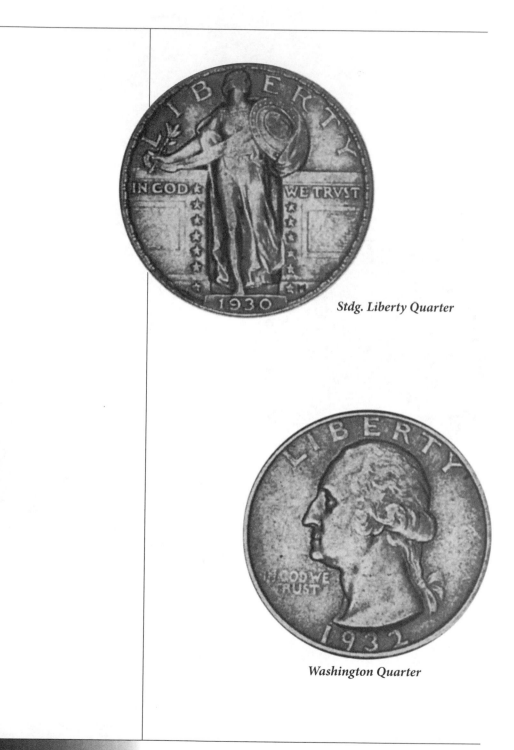

Stdg. Liberty Quarter

Washington Quarter

Coin Collecting 101

Wlkg. Liberty Half

Morgan Dollar

Barber Coins

Very Fine

VF-20 (very fine)—*Coins reflect noticeable wear at the fine points in the design, though they may remain sharp overall. Although the details will be slightly smoothed, all lettering and major features must remain sharp.*

Indian cent: All letters in "LIBERTY" complete but worn; headdress shows considerable flatness, with flat spots on tips of feathers.

Lincoln cent: Hair, cheek, jaw and bow-tie details will be worn but clearly separated, and wheat stalks on the reverse will be full, with no weak spots.

Buffalo nickel: High spots on hair braid and cheek will be flat but show more detail, and a full horn will remain on the buffalo.

Jefferson nickel: Well over half of the major hair detail will remain, and the pillars on Monticello will remain well defined, with triangular roof partially visible.

Mercury dime: Hair braid will show some detail, and three-quarters of the details will remain in the feathers. The two diagonal bands on the fasces will show completely, but be worn smooth at the middle, with the vertical lines sharp.

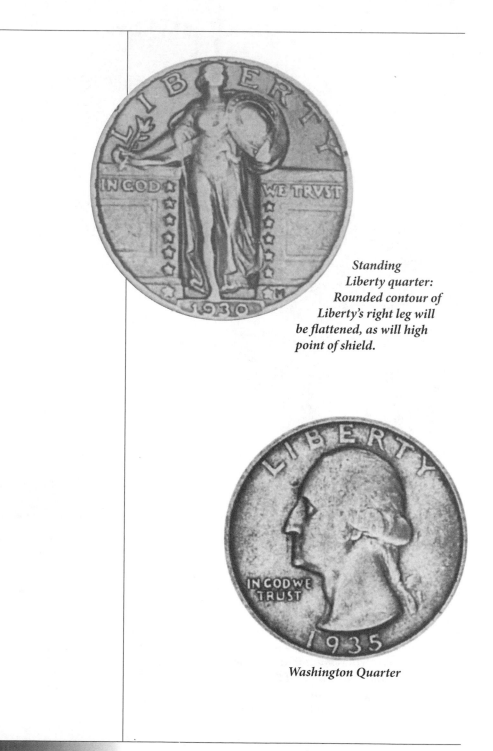

Standing Liberty quarter: Rounded contour of Liberty's right leg will be flattened, as will high point of shield.

Washington Quarter

Walking Liberty half dollar: All lines of the skirt will show but be worn on high points, and over half of the feathers will show on eagle.

Morgan dollar: Two-thirds of hairlines from forehead to ear must show, and ear will be well defined, while feathers on eagle's breast may be worn smooth.

Barber coins: All seven letters of "LIBERTY" on headband must stand out sharply, while head wreath will be well outlined top to bottom.

Fine

F-12 (fine)—*This is the most widely collected condition. Coins show evidence of moderate to considerable but generally even wear on all high points, though all elements of the design and lettering remain bold. Where "LIBERTY" appears on the headband, it must be fully visible. The rim must be fully raised and sharp on 20th-century coins.*

Indian Cent

Lincoln Cent

Buffalo Nickel

Jefferson Nickel

Mercury Dime

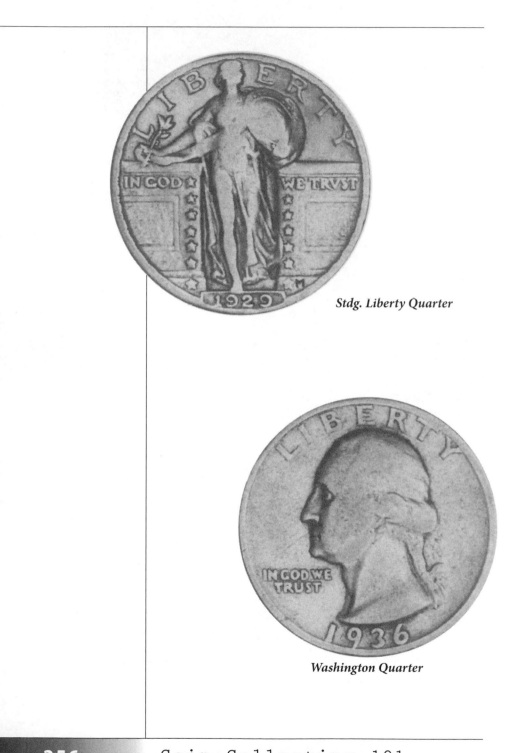

Stdg. Liberty Quarter

Washington Quarter

Coin Collecting 101

Wlkg. Liberty Half

Morgan Dollar

Barber Coins

Very Good

VG-8 (very good)—*Coins show considerable wear, with most of the points of detail worn nearly smooth. At least three letters must show where "LIBERTY" appears in a headband. On 20th-century coinage, the rim is starting to merge with the lettering.*

Indian Cent

Lincoln Cent

Buffalo Nickel

Jefferson Nickel

Mercury Dime

Stdg. Liberty Quarter

Washington Quarter

Wlkg. Liberty Half

Morgan Dollar

Barber Coins

Good

G-4 (good)—In this condition, only the basic design detail remains distinguishable in outline form, with all points of detail being worn smooth. "LIBERTY" has disappeared, and rims are nearly merging with the lettering.

Indian Cent

Lincoln Cent

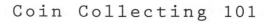

Buffalo Nickel

Jefferson Nickel

Mercury Dime

Stdg. Liberty Quarter

Washington Quarter

Coin Collecting 101

Wlkg. Liberty Half

Morgan Dollar

Barber Coins

About good or fair—*A coin identifiable by date and mint but otherwise badly worn, with only parts of the lettering showing. Such coins are of value to collectors only as space fillers and command a significant premium only in cases of extreme scarcity.*

Proof—*Created as collector coins, proof specimens are struck on specially selected planchets with highly polished dies and generally display a mirrorlike finish, sometimes featuring frosted highlight areas. All individual proof valuations listed in this guide are for superb Proof-65 specimens.*

Prooflike and deep-mirror prooflike—*These terms describe the degree of reflectiveness and cameo contrast on well-struck Morgan dollars. A DMPL coin may appear to be a proof at first glance, and a prooflike specimen has a lesser (but still considerable) degree of flash. Bag marks are more noticeable on PL and DMPL Morgans. Some common dates are scarce in this condition.*

Note: The exact description of circulated grades varies widely from issue to issue, so the preceding is a general summary only. For a more detailed description of the grades and grading methods, purchase the latest edition of the Official ANA Grading Standards for United States Coins by the American Numismatic Association.

This is the end. I hope that you won't put this book away and never open it again. Like the talking car in a recent TV commercial, this book should be consulted on a frequent basis. There are pieces of advice that you may need to be reminded of or ideas that you want to follow up on. If you have questions, by all means get in touch with me and I'll be glad to help.

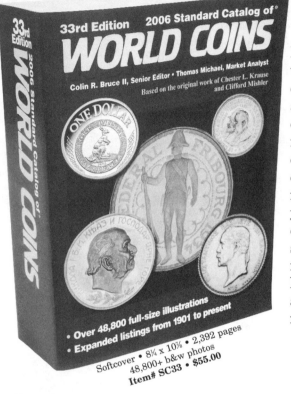

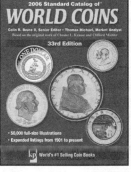